W9-AYE-842

GUERRILLA KINDNESS

A Manual of Good Works,
Kind Acts and
Thoughtful Deeds

Gavin Whitsett

Impact Publishers®
San Luis Obispo, California 93406

Copyright © 1993
Gavin C. Whitsett

All rights reserved under International and Pan-American Copyright Conventions. No part of this book may be reproduced, stored in a retrieval system, or transmitted in any form or by any means, electronic, mechanical, photocopying, recording or otherwise, without express written permission of the author or publisher, except for brief quotations in critical reviews.

Library of Congress Cataloging-in-Publication Data

Whitsett, Gavin C.
    Guerrilla kindness: a manual of good works, kind acts and thoughtful
deeds / Gavin Whitsett.
        p.   cm.
    Includes bibliographical references.
    ISBN 0-915166-79-8 (alk. paper)
    1. Kindness.   2. Etiquette.   I. Title
BJ1533.K5W45   1993
177'.7—dc20   93-20506
                                                        CIP

Cover design by Emilie Kong, North Hollywood, California
Printed in the United States of America

Published by **Impact** ⬙ **Publishers**®
                POST OFFICE BOX 1094
        SAN LUIS OBISPO, CALIFORNIA 93406

CONTENTS

ACKNOWLEDGEMENTS

The kindness of strangers buoyed me early and often in life. Way before researchers established the fact, I learned that people are good. My thanks go first to those strangers.

My colleagues and students at the University of Southern Indiana, Southern Illinois University, and Western Kentucky University — especially Dr. Joe Stearns, Dr. Tom Pace, Dr. Richard Lanigan, Dr. Jim Blevins, Dr. Helen Sands, Mary Schroeder, Cookie Doherty, jo hummel, Brian Williams and Dr. Dal Herring — all helped support my development as a Kindness Guerrilla.

Of course, everyone at Patchwork Central contributed to *Guerrilla Kindness*. I want to thank especially Jean Beckman, Eileen Brittain, Mary Frances Cease, Becca Conrad, Ruth Doyle, Don and CeCe Goerlitz, Jill and Bill Hemminger, Judi Jacobson, Nelia and Calvin Kimbrough, Mary MacGregor, Deborah McBride, Bill Morrison, Ed and Marion Ouellette, Susan Steinkamp, Beth Stone, Helen Templeton, and Maggie Zopf.

Anne Herbert invented the slogan that ignited my interest in Guerrilla Kindness: "Practice random kindness and senseless acts of beauty." The idea for this book was hatched subsequently in conversations with my friend Robert Weidman. And Alan Winslow's love and enthusiasm sustained me when my optimism for this project dimmed.

I dedicate *Guerrilla Kindness* to my family and, most especially, Kathy Workman.

INTRODUCTION

*When I look back at my experience of being confronted with
death and ask myself what, in that hour, were the
memories I treasured, I have little difficulty in answering. I
cared not at all for my personal success.... What I did care
about were the thoughts that I had made a few happier,
that I had done a few kindnesses, that I had won some love.*
— Arthur Christopher Benson

It's late fall... I'm driving out to school... admiring the leaves... just another easy morning.

Suddenly I catch the message on the car ahead and, jolted awake, I leap out of my morning daze and into the most delightful and absorbing fantasy... my imagination soaring! It's just a bumper sticker, but the words trigger a rush of excitement and wonder. What do they mean?

"PRACTICE RANDOM ACTS OF KINDNESS"

Random kindness? The idea didn't compute. I had visions of strangers spontaneously reaching out to help strangers... acting anonymously... without recognition or reward. I saw masses of people giving favors to those who hadn't earned them... or giving in greater measure than was deserved. I imagined a world where everyone lightened up; where foolishness was fun; where helpfulness replaced selfishness; where kindnesses were traded freely without anyone keeping score.

Random kindness seems foolish on one level. This is supposed to be a materialistic, ME FIRST society, isn't it? Practicing random kindness doesn't make sense (or cents). But practicing random kindness does make sense... good sense... to many of us. We've found that unexpected kindnesses gently shake both givers and recipients out of the business-as-usual, ME FIRST way of viewing one another. Plus, one kind deed frequently prompts ripple kindnesses. For the first time since the 60's, a growing underground is challenging the wisdom of the ME FIRST view with an alternative, THEE FIRST approach. Indeed, the divergence of the ME FIRST and THEE FIRST camps is producing a new generation of revolutionaries: people dedicated to warming the globe with kindness, courtesy, frivolity, and beauty — a principle I call *Guerrilla Kindness.*

The course of human history is determined by what takes
place in our hearts

— anonymous

Like guerrillas, we strike against materialism, against strangers' indifference toward strangers, and against the ME FIRST orientation of America's Establishment. Unlike guerrillas, though, our arms are for hugging; our weapons are kinds looks, kind words, and kind deeds. And the Establishment we've targeted isn't a They. It's We. It's our own brothers and sisters. It is ourselves. Our only enemies are the indifferent and uncharitable spirits which clamor within us all and compete with our impulses to give and love and play and care. And we believe we can change things.

The reasonable man adapts himself to the world; the
unreasonable one persists in trying to adapt the world to
himself. Therefore all progress depends on the
unreasonable man.

— George Bernard Shaw

The good news is that our revolution doesn't require us to change human nature. The capacity for kindness is built into our genes just as solidly as our capacity for selfishness. We need only to listen and follow the kindhearted impulses that already come to us. The majority of Americans want to be kind but have forgotten how to listen and respond to those impulses.

Guerrilla Kindness will illuminate some of the infinite opportunities you have to strike a blow for humanity and for your own deep-down goodness. Here you'll find hundreds of acts, ideas, and tips — all to remind you how you can act on the charitable impulses you have each day.

Guerrilla Kindness celebrates life and the many ways you can shake-up your corner of the world with unexpected kindness, playfulness, and beauty. I hope that reading about the possibilities makes you want to jump into the game too. Using the ideas you find here to become a Kindness Guerrilla, *you can make a difference that makes a difference.*

> *Never doubt that a small group of thoughtful citizens can change the world. Indeed, it's the only thing that ever has.*
> — Margaret Mead

GUERRILLA WORKS

- Bury nickels in the park. Slip them into the sand beneath swings and sliding boards so kids will discover Buried Treasure! Bury them a bit deeper at randomly chosen spots in the park so people with metal detectors will find them.

- Throw an UnBirthday for someone you want to do something especially nice for. An UnBirthday is just like a real birthday — surprise party, friends, cake, and presents — except it's not the person's birthday. Darline and Cory use it as a great excuse to shower a friend with love and have fun at the same time.

- Few kindnesses are more fun or produce more delight: take your Polaroid out to public places, make photos of happy-looking couples, and give them the pictures! I got my first Polaroid more than 20 years ago, and now I take it to fairs, sports events, celebrations and parks... wherever there are large groups of folks having fun.

• Terri has established a routine of making the last thing she says to her children at night a compliment, a thank you, or some other statement of appreciation. She whispers it privately to Aaron and Jennifer as she tucks each child in.

• When you catch others in the act of making the world a better place — picking up litter, helping others, or saying a kind word — let them know they've been seen, and thank them. I met a dear friend this way. She was so pleased to be noticed because, as she told me, she makes a conscious effort to brighten others' days. We began talking about our mutual interest in kindness-as-a-hobby, and it was with Lee that I first used the phrase "Guerrilla Kindness."

• If a friend is wrestling with rough times, tell her, "I want to be your 911! Call me anytime you want to talk. Promise?"

• Become somebody's Secret Pal. Pick someone who played a positive role sometime in your past, an acquaintance you admire but don't know well, or a complete stranger. Every few weeks send a treat of some kind: a gift certificate to a bakery, theatre tickets, a whimsical toy, or a coupon for a free car wash.

GUERRILLA TIP

Each day, do something that doesn't compute.

When we do a kindness without any regard for recognition or reward, when we inconvenience ourselves and freely give part of ourselves away, we challenge the every-man-for-himself logic of the world.

Unconditional courtesy defies the conventional moral that rudeness is a fair response to rudeness and that courteous treatment should be reserved for those who are courteous to us.

Let's advance the revolution against so-called "common sense"... act in ways that the establishment may see as foolish and illogical... day by day by day.

• If kids are waiting in line behind you when you buy an ice cream cone from a street vendor, buy one for each of them too.

• Give of yourself. Make room in your life for regular volunteer work at a nursing home, a local food pantry, a nature preserve, a recycling center, or some other group that needs you.

• "Record the names, addresses, and phone numbers of neighbors on all 4 sides of you." That was the advice Officer Kimbrough gave our Neighborhood Watch group. Keep the list near the phone. If an emergency occurs, you'll be able to tell the 911 operator the information necessary to send help right away.

• Kids love to launch balloons. Whenever there are free helium balloons from some advertising promotion, Mrs. O is not bashful about taking as many as they'll give her. Then she gives them to kids with permission to "hold on to this for one minute then LET IT FLY!" (She also encourages the kids to pick up litter, to more-than-make-up-for the balloons they scatter.)

• When you've got a carload of youngsters and have to get gas, have the whole gang pile out of the car and wash the windshields of all the other motorists who are fueling up.

GUERRILLA TIP

Act when stressed.

The best antidote for stress is what noted researcher Hans Selye calls "altruistic egoism." Cultivating goodwill, behaving courteously, and saying kind things — all help activate our body's relaxation response.

If stuck in a traffic jam or a long line at the store, use your time to dream up something kind you can say or do to surprise another. The calming effect of thinking kind thoughts and doing kind deeds has been thoroughly confirmed in over 40 years of psychological research.

> *You make people happy and you bring happiness to your-self when you do unexpected acts of kindness without fan-fare and without thought of reward.*
>
> — Marcus Bach

- Bill improved the odds he'll be able to play the Good Samaritan on the road by preparing to be kind. He placed one of those plastic milk crates in his trunk to carry flares, a fire extinguisher, jumper cables, engine starting fluid, a can of Fix-A-Flat, duct tape, Vice-Grip pliers, and a flashlight.

- It's the core of Gandhi's revolutionary message, and there must be something to it. All of history's great peacemakers have tried to teach us the same powerful lesson: TREAT PEOPLE LIKE THEY ALREADY ARE WHAT THEY WISH TO BE. Reasonable. Fair. Good. Give others the benefit of the doubt by assuming they intend well even if their actions sometimes appear to be mean-spirited.

- Support your Humane Society. Volunteers and poorly paid staff work long hours to reduce the suffering of our fellow travelers.

- If there are long lines at the check-out counter and another register opens, let those in front of you move to the new register first. Similarly, if people behind you in line have only a few items to buy, let them in the line ahead of you.

- Join the Guerrilla Greens by planting flowers, shrubs, and trees in public places. Carol and John broadcast beauty in public places by buying dozens of spring bulbs when they go on sale. Crocus and daffodils are favorites. They have fun burying them randomly in parks and other patches of public ground.

- I like to leave beauty marks in spots with high visibility, so I plant flowers along roadsides. For those places that are mowed, crown vetch thrives on the barbering. Road banks that don't get mowed but do get plenty of sun are great for black-eyed susans and daylillies; scatter columbine seeds on shady roadsides.

- Or, follow my friend Veronica's example, and plant a tree in a nearby park each year. With municipal Parks Departments receiving less funding each year, nobody is going to be too upset if you avoid red tape by just not telling the Parks Department. Plant your donation to the neighborhood in an oversized hole, stake it with 3 stakes, wrap the trunk with protective paper, and faithfully water. The early fall is the best time to plant. River birches grow amazingly fast; oaks shelter many generations; and hawthorns are tough, sport beautiful white flowers in the spring, and attract birds with their bright red berries in the fall and winter.

• Another tip: churches, schools, and libraries may be receptive to your offer to plant beautiful things on their grounds too.

• You can still brighten your corner of the world even if you don't have the time or energy for heavy duty gardening. Plant groups of peonies, oriental poppies, daylillies, iris, and phlox. Because they're perennials they'll come back year after year. And with this combination, you'll have at least one group in glorious bloom from May to September.

• Our own star! Jan — one of Kathy's sisters — named a star for us when we got married. You too can make others feel special by naming stars for them. The Ministry of Star Registration (1-800-544-8814) will record the name in their archives and send the recipient a sky map to find the star.

• Volunteer to be Mr/Ms Fix-It for an elderly neighbor. Many of the routine household chores the rest of us can easily handle are too much for some older folks. Changing light bulbs, replacing faucet washers, tightening loose screws, and raising or lowering storm windows can all be part of your ministry of kindness.

GUERRILLA TIP

Spend 17 minutes a day on kindness.

Medical authority Allan Luks recently published some surprising discoveries about the "healing power of doing good."

Luks shows that there's substantial medical evidence that acting kindly produces health benefits remarkably similar to those we enjoy from exercise programs. People who regularly help others develop stronger immune systems, improved cardiovascular circulation, a heightened sense of well-being, and even live longer.

Two hours a week — 17 minutes a day — of kind behavior seem to produce the most significant results.

- Make a point of recalling specific kindnesses your parents did for you when you were young. Describe the event for them and let them know you treasure the memory.

- Your lawn doesn't have to rival the fairways at Pebble Beach. The fertilizers, weed killers, insecticides, and millions of gallons of water people use to have picture-perfect lawns are major causes of ecological destruction. Give a care for the earth our children will inherit, and don't buy into the hype the chemical industry has sold your neighbors.

- Write and propose a toast to your hosts at a dinner party. Or deliver a toast to a special guest at your own dinner party.

- Take the time to make expectations clear. Tell others what you expect from them and ask what they expect from you. If meeting each other's expectations is an important part of your relationship, this small step can avert a lot of hurt.

- Search for opportunities for others to shine. Assign tasks or make requests that will give others the chance to display their talents.

GUERRILLA TIP

Make your 27,248 days count.

That's about as long as actuary tables predict most people will live: 74.6 years. What would your priorities be if you knew you had only one year. Or what would be important to you if you found out you had just seven days left? How would you treat people? Doesn't it make sense to adopt those same attitudes for the long run?

When death, the great reconciler, has come, it is never our
tenderness that we repent of, but our severity.
— George Elliot

• A proven method of teaching children empathy: have them use their imaginations to guess how others might be feeling. When reading to your child, for example, occasionally stop and ask, "What is Charlotte feeling now? Why do you think she may feel that way?"

• Don's father planted and maintained a garden at a local nursing home. Except for the folks at the home, no one knew he had done it. "He never told us. And because it was all perennials, it wasn't like he had to mysteriously disappear every weekend to care for his project. The head of the nursing home called us after he had read that Dad had passed away. He wanted us to know of Dad's selfless gift."

• Touch hungry! Anthropologist Ashley Montagu has found that all humans crave physical contact. And most of us don't get enough of it.

• Take advantage of every "socially approved" opportunity to touch others. Besides shaking hands, most people will appreciate a brief, light pat on the upper arm — one of the few other "O.K." ways to touch other people.

GORILLA KINDNESS

The compassion that you see in kindhearted creatures is
God's compassion; he has given it to them to protect the
helpless

— Sri Ramakrishna

In a mountain of muscle and coal black hair, a kitten purrs contentedly as she is lovingly stroked by the most famous great ape in the world. The giant is Koko. The kitten is her dearest companion in the world.

Scientists at Stanford University have studied Koko for more than fifteen years. In that time, she has learned sign language and regularly uses over 400 gestures — some of which she made up herself — to describe her thoughts and feelings to her human companions.

The study of gorillas in captivity and in the wild can teach us a lot about the nature of primate kindness — whether it be the gorilla or guerrilla variety. Simply observing gorilla kindness leads to insights into the core of guerrilla kindness.

Gorillas are the largest primates. They weigh from 400 to 600 pounds and can reach six feet in height. With chests measuring five-and-a-half feet and arm spans of nine feet, gorillas are enormously muscular. The powerful apes are capable of bending tempered steel bars two inches thick!

And yet humanity's closest living relatives are quiet and retiring. Peaceful vegetarians, gorillas rarely fight. When tensions between them do develop, they find ways to reduce conflict in nonviolent ways: usually by roaring and beating their chests.

The kindness with which Koko cares for her kitten is typical of gorillas. In the wild, gorillas routinely protect the elderly, the sick, and the young — even those who are not their own — and the scientists who've lived among the great apes (Dian Fossey, who inspired the film, *Gorillas In The Mist,* for example) are unanimous in their admiration for the animals' benevolence.

Like the mighty gorilla, Kindness Guerrillas don't *have* to be kind. Our soft revolution aims instead to scramble the "might is right" social order. Gorillas don't keep ledgers of those to whom kindness is due and in what measure it's due. Neither do we. Koko and her brethren in the wild obviously don't structure their lives with the ME FIRST logic that is practically an institution in our human society. And the selfless altruism for which the gentle giants are known parallels our own campaign to act without expectations of recognition or reward.

So in many ways the great ape is a model of how each of us aspires to behave. The gorilla/guerrilla homophone is intentional in Guerrilla Kindness. Just as gorillas break the "rules" and confound the expectations we might have of such intelligent and powerful beasts, we guerrillas do things that, hopefully, will bring so-called common sense up for discussion and critical review.

GUERRILLA WORKS

• Let 'em ride! When you buy tickets for a ride at the fair, buy several extra. Give them to kids when the ride is over and let them enjoy a second go-round.

• Post that impulse with Post-It brand note pads by 3M. They stick anywhere, are small enough to fit in a pocket, purse, or glove compartment, and are just the thing to leave spontaneous compliments or cheerful messages to brighten the days of neighbors, friends, and strangers.

• Spend an evening at an interstate bus terminal with the aim of kindly responding to whatever needs you observe. The Travelers' Aid posts that used to be in every train or bus depot have long been out of business, but the need is still there.

• Pay the Social Security of your household help so they'll have an income when they retire. (Incidentally, it's the law.)

• Cheer up friends who need a diversion with a joke, card trick, or magic stunt. Here's one: Tell your audience to "(1) pick any number and don't tell me, (2) double it, (3) add 4 to it, (4) divide it in half, (5) subtract the number you originally had from what you have now, and (6) *you have 2 left over.*" (The remainder will always be half the number you add in step 3.)

• Find something positive and enthusiastic to say about the things others are planning to do. It's a joy when others care enough about us and what makes us happy to be as excited as we are. When a friend is positively hopping up and down with anticipation, open your eyes and mouth real wide, hold hands, and bounce up and down on the balls of your feet.

• When you receive good service, ask for the server's full name. Write the company president and tell him or her about the attentive and capable employee who waited on you.

This is especially fun because when you ask to see the manager to get the company president's name and address, you get everybody's' attention. Then, when you explain why you want to contact the president, the server gets to bask in the warmth of the whole crew's admiration.

GUERRILLA TIP

See the Light.

Gandhi is said to have been so effective at making people feel good about themselves because he always saw the internal, spiritual goodness in others rather than the world-weary, prejudiced, and often hostile exteriors.

When interacting with others, we can make them feel special by seeing through their Public Selves and focusing on the internal light all of us possess. By recognizing and addressing others' Internal Light... their essential goodness... we affirm that at their core is a person worthy of kindness and affection: a spiritual brother or sister.

- When I was a carpenter, I helped build a house on Martha's Vineyard for a man who had accumulated enormous power and wealth. Every day Mr. Simon would drop by to see how the work was going, and — this is why I will always remember him — he always treated the physical laborers with warmth and respect. He acted as if we were as important as he was.

Wes, an executive with a large corporation, is also among the most courteous people I know. He always lets others go through doors before him, for example. Regardless of whether they're young or old, male or female, stranger or friend, Wes holds the door and gestures for others to precede him.

I've found that most extraordinarily successful people are like that. Mr. Simon, Wes and others I've met remind me of the saying "No one is too big to be kind, but some are too small." The kindness of these "big" men doesn't fit the stereotype of the blustery tycoon, does it?

Remind yourself daily that there are no little people. Try to really "see" the human being in the role each is assigned to perform, and engage each person with the courtesy and hearty good cheer with which you greet your dearest acquaintances.

GUERRILLA TIP

Hug and run.

Like the Lone Ranger, gallop away after bestowing your gifts. It helps relieve the wariness strangers may feel by showing them that you (a) don't desire a long interaction, (b) don't expect anything from them in return, and (c) have no motive other than simple charity.

And some of the most pleasing kindnesses, of course, are those we perform unseen. Putting a flower on a stranger's car and then leaving, for example. Truly the work of a guerrilla!

> *A little kindness wrought unseen;*
> *I know not whose love's tribute paid;*
> *I only know that it has made*
> *Life's pathways smoother, life's borders green.*
>
> — anonymous

- Self-help books. There are some great ones on the market these days. Some of the best have to do with beating depression. And — have you noticed? — all the experts agree that one of the most effective ways to lift your spirits is to focus your attention on others rather than on yourself.

- Here's a Guerrilla Work that is as pleasing to others as it is helpful for you: BE THE FIRST TO NOTICE when others have changed their hair styles, visited the tanning salon, lost weight, bought new glasses, or put on new outfits. Your attentiveness will brighten the day for you both!

- My Mom is one of the most gracious people I know. She says that when you've been entertained in another's home, one way to make your host feel especially good is to offer a compliment about the house or apartment right before you leave. Try a phrase that begins, "You know, something I've been admiring all evening is...."

- Count to ten. Research reveals that when we react angrily to others, our initial burst of anger lasts only about seven seconds. You can stop unloading on others and spare yourself the pain of trying to undo the irreversible effects of your eruptions if you follow this ancient curative.

• Guerrilla Works satisfy a deep down need in us revolutionaries. Noted psychologist Abraham Maslow called it the need for self- actualization: the yearning to be all that we can be. Some people join the army. Some go back to school. Some make New Year's resolutions.

On New Year's Eve 1990, my nephew Henry resolved to say a kind word to every "clean-up person" he saw. Henry had briefly worked as a janitor when he was laid off his regular job, and he appreciated how much work and how little reward there was in cleaning up other people's messes.

Henry carried his pledge like a prayer, just in the back of his mind, and found that he automatically glanced around for maintenance people everywhere he went. He discovered that "the invisible people aren't invisible if you really try to see them." When he saw a busboy or janitor or clean-up crew, he would greet them with "Thanks for always keeping the place looking so sharp."

Although New Year's Eve 1990 is ancient history now, Henry still looks for and compliments clean-up people. His routine, performed humbly and without fanfare, helps him satisfy and stay mindful of his need for self-actualization. Or in Henry's words, "I'm not any smarter than I was in 1990. I'm not any richer. I'm not stronger or better looking than I was then. But I am kinder."

Be all you can be. Compliment and thank the clean-up people in your world.

• Make money while you campaign for a kinder, cleaner world by buying shares in socially responsible mutual funds. Funds like Calvert Social Investment and Pax World funds don't invest in companies with discriminatory hiring practices, poor worker health and safety records, records of environmental pollution, or firms that manufacture weapons, tobacco, or alcohol. Pax World has recently achieved a three year average total return of 18.5% versus 13.5% returned by the average equity fund.

• Stick it to friends who are moving away. Before Phil and Elaine left town, their best friends filled a box with adhesives: Elmer's Glue, electrical tape, duct tape, super glue, Post-It notes, plastic suction cups with hooks, Liquid Nails, silicone sealer, Scotch tape, and epoxy glue. They included a note, sealed the box, and wrote "Don't open til you get there." When Phil and Elaine opened the mystery box, they found their friends' note: "Even though you've moved, LET'S STICK TOGETHER!"

• Be the last to board the bus at your stop. In addition to paying your own fare, tell the driver you want to anonymously pay the fare of the first passenger to board at the next stop.

GUERRILLA TIP

Define your mission.

Researchers who've studied helping behavior among strangers have found that the people most likely to respond to others in need are those with a definite sense of social responsibility. That is, those who have made a deliberate decision to help strangers are most apt to actually do so when they're needed.

You will improve the odds of treating others kindly if you'll stop now and answer the question, "In what ways do I want to act like a Kindness Guerrilla?" You may decide you want to remember others' birthdays. Maybe you want to be extra alert for opportunities to be a courteous driver. Or perhaps you will decide to always find something about which to compliment waitresses.

Defining your mission will help you sustain your campaign to contribute to global warming.

• An original poem is one of the most thoughtful, touching gifts you can offer. And it makes any occasion extra special. Anyone can write a "Roses are red...." four liner. QUALITY HERE DOES NOT MATTER! It's your taking the time to do it that will make the receiver feel genuinely cared for.

• House-sit for neighbors who'll be away. Offer to water the plants, feed the fish, bring in the mail and newspapers, turn the lights on and off randomly, and call them immediately if there is a problem. Your neighbors can enjoy their trip without having to worry about things at home.

• Ask people questions you think they would enjoy answering. That's the guerrilla tactic Nancy uses. The most gifted conversationalist I know, Nancy says everyone has a Hot Button — some topic they love to talk about. It can be a hobby, a career goal, an upcoming trip, a favorite memory, a social cause to which they're committed, or any other area of personal interest.

• Give other drivers a brake. When others wish to get out of side streets or into your lane of traffic, stop and wave them in.

GUERRILLA TIP

Don't leave it for the other guy.

"I thought someone else would help" is one of the most frequent excuses from those who witnessed a need for kindness and did not respond. Probably all of us have read of tragedies in which no one stepped forward to help because everyone thought that someone else — "the other guy" — would take care of it.
BE THE OTHER GUY!

> *Responsibility, n. A detachable burden easily shifted to the shoulders of God, Fate, Fortune, Luck, or one's neighbor. In the days of astrology it was customary to unload it upon a star.*
>
> — Ambrose Bierce

- Look for clues to others' Hot Buttons in their physical features, clothing, jewelry, body language, casual comments, what they're carrying, what they're doing, or where they are. Or, just ask. "What do you like to do when you're not working?" is good bait for conversation fishing.

- Honesty is not the best policy. Love is. When an honest response might unnecessarily hurt another, don't say it.

- Revive the pleasure of simple snuggling in your intimate relationship. Instead of reducing touch to just pre-sex routine, practice Non-Demand Snuggling. Hold each other in whatever way feels most comfortable for 20 minutes or so. If you become sexually aroused, fine; enjoy it but don't have sex. It's the pleasure of cuddling for cuddling's sake.

- Buying illegal drugs supports brutal drug lords and systematic violence in the countries where those drugs are produced. Kindness Guerrillas just say "no".

- Sport a bumper sticker that celebrates life, love, and laughter.

THE GOOD NEWS ABOUT THE KINDNESS OF HUMANS

*The ability to give kindness and receive appreciation in
return in the one thing which really proves that man has
climbed up out of the jungle and gotten hold of something
higher that just the satisfaction of survival.*
— Joseph C. Harsch

A persistent theme in Western thought is that mankind has tumbled away from its original state of perfection. Human history, in the popular view, is the record of a naturally selfish animal driven by evil desires, appetites, and impulses.

Nowadays most people still view humankind pessimistically. One recent survey found that 46% of those interviewed agreed with statements such as "Most people are just out for themselves." And many people are sharply cynical about our future. A full 60% of people contacted in another survey believed that war can never be eliminated because savagery is an inevitable consequence of human nature.

The consensus regarding our innate wickedness was so firmly established that it wasn't until the 60's that the bright side of human nature — helping, caring, and sharing — was scientifically studied. Now we know that the dark view of human nature is wrong.

Hundreds of studies have disproved the proposition that men and women are only out for themselves. In *Human Aggression*, Robert Baron summarizes 300 research projects that indicate aggression in no more innate than human kindness. And numerous other experiments, conducted in both laboratory and natural settings, confirm the fact that most people will go out of their way to help strangers who need help. Kindness is an integral part of human nature.

Consider also General S. L. A. Marshall's discovery that during World War II, the majority of American soldiers refused to kill, refused even to fire their weapons at enemy positions. Or these statistics: almost 90% of Americans give money to charitable organizations, and close to 50% regularly donate their time for volunteer work with such groups. These volunteers work an average of nearly 5 hours a week.

While it may not jibe with so-called "common sense," the truth is that most people are good.

> *It is to the credit of human nature that...it loves more than it hates.*
>
> — Nathaniel Hawthorne

GUERRILLA WORKS

- Anticipate what would comfort, delight, or help out your friend in an upcoming situation. Whether it's a job interview, a medical procedure, the arrival of house guests, or the day they will hear some big news, your remembering will mean a lot. An offer to help, a small gift, or just a phone call says "What's important to you is important to me!"

- Calvin displays photographs of the people he loves. The pictures are everywhere — at home and where he works — and I must admit I always look to see if there's one of me in his collection. Especially dear friends will be touched to see their photo on your wall or desk when they visit your home or office.
  (And, oh yes. There is always one of me. Thanks, Calvin!)

- Keep a gift file. When friends mention some item they recently saw and liked, put the idea in your file before you forget it. Your file is also the place to store those random ideas that come to you: treats, surprises, and other kind impulses you can someday use to cheer a friend.

- Refer to information others have shared with you in previous conversations. Your comment will show that you think what they say is worth remembering. If you're scheduling a lunch date, say, pencil in some key words when you write the date in your appointment book. Something like "Ask about Rhonda's surgery."

GUERRILLA TIP

Let it be.

Sometimes your kindness will flop. Others will rebuff you and you'll feel foolish. Or your well-intended word or deed will frighten, hurt, or offend the other person. That's when you need to be kind to yourself. Accept what's past is past; take whatever lesson there may be for you in the experience; and then bounce back. Even the angels stumble, you know, and the world needs your humble ministry more than ever.

What you say to yourself now is critically important here. Don't catastrophize — that is, don't blow the incident out of proportion. Do remind yourself of the good things you do. Do accept that, okay, sometimes you make mistakes. "I'm disappointed in how that worked out," you might tell yourself, "but I do many other kind things that do work out. If I want to lighten up on others, to allow them to make mistakes, I must be willing to lighten up on myself."

• When you mail your payment to a tradesman who has done good work or helped you out of a jam, include a simple note of thanks. Most plumbers, electricians, carpenters and such hear more gripes than praise, and your warm words will help them feel proud of themselves.

• Ride with the police. Make arrangements through the Chief's office to spend a Friday evening accompanying officers as they respond to calls. Your empathy for both the police and the troubled people they try to help will get a substantial boost.

• When you see a person with a disabled vehicle, are you wary of stopping and getting involved with strangers? One way to both assist others and protect yourself is to stop and volunteer to call for help at the next phone booth in the direction you're traveling. You don't even have to get out of your own car. A tip: note the first highway mile marker you see so you can tell whomever you call where to find the stranded motorists.

• Have you noticed that many people are not comfortable responding to compliments? Follow compliments with questions so others will have an easier time knowing what to say in response to your kind words: "Those are neat earrings. Where did you find them?"

GUERRILLA TIP

Act at once.

Most kindhearted impulses cool quickly, Be willing to temporarily suspend what you're in the middle of and immediately do the kind deed that just popped into your head. Noticing and readily responding to kind impulses will also dramatically increase the number of impulses that come to you.

If there is a key to becoming a Kindness Guerrilla — and I believe there is — it is the willingness to act on kind impulses the moment they arise!

*I expect to pass through life but once. If therefore, there
be any kindness I can show, or any good thing I can do to
any fellow being, let me do it now, and not defer or neglect
it, as I shall not pass this way again.*

— William Penn

- When Nelia spots a yard that is particularly well cared for — lots of flowering bushes, trees, and other plants, for example — she notes the address and sends an appreciative postcard to "Dear Beauty Lover."

- If a friend has bad breath, buy your friend a pack of mints or gum. Gently encourage him or her to use them. I drink coffee and smoke a pipe; I also like to stand close to people when I talk to them. During my first year as a teacher, a student was brave enough to let me know my breath was toxic. Most other people will want to know too!

  Likewise, if people to whom you're talking have crumbs on their faces, unbuttoned buttons, or open zippers, TELL THEM!

- There are dozens of pleasant-looking people I seem to run into everywhere — at school, at the fitness center, at the grocery. I don't really want to take the time to have conversations, but I do want to communicate that I recognize and have some fondness for them.

  I've worked out what seems to be a satisfactory solution by developing and using affectionate nicknames for those I like but don't really know. I use "Mighty Man" for a young man in a wheel chair; I see him frequently and marvel at the size and strength of his arms. You may see people for whom you could use "Lady-With-The-Nice-Smile" or "Wonder Kid." Then, it's a simple matter of saying something like "Hello, Lady-With-The-Nice-Smile" as you pass.

• I expect to be arrested any day now because I've discovered the thrill of being a Graffiti Guerrilla. I use sidewalk chalk to write messages of peace and love on heavily traveled walkways. Though I've done it for years, I still expect the "authorities" to have me detained for questioning. It's a relief when I see that with the very first drop of rain, the evidence completely disappears.

• Sharon and Becca want to remind people to lighten up and enjoy life. They put their positive messages on public bulletins boards, kiosks, and telephone poles. Their brilliant silk-screened posters are seen by hundreds every day.

• You too can become a Graffiti Guerrilla and blanket the town with messages of good cheer. *Use only washable markers* like water-color pens and sidewalk chalk, then start scribbling, doodling, and drawing. Make up your own statements or use one of these:
* *There is not a shred of evidence that life is supposed to be serious.*
* *No one is a failure who is enjoying life.*
* *The secret of life is enjoy the passage of time.*
* *Life is uncertain. Eat dessert first.*
* *All the animals except man know that the main business of life is to enjoy it.*
* *The world is your playground. Why aren't you playing?*
And, for highbrows,
* *Gaudeamus Igitur* (Latin for "Let's celebrate!").
(A terrific source of positive messages is Allen Klein's *Quotations To Cheer You Up When The World Is Getting You Down*, $9.95 from Sterling Publishing).

- Mimi makes kids feel like real people. Because kids love getting mail addressed to just them, she writes letters to the children she knows — even if they're just next door. Mimi includes stamped, self-addressed envelopes in her letters, and she asks the kids to write her back.

- It's a good thing Clark walks on the right side of the law. He'd make a heckuva pickpocket! When visitors prepare to leave his home or office, he slips rolls of sugar free mints into their coats, purses, or pockets. We know he's going to do it, but we've never caught him in the act.

- Write a Letter To An Editor thanking every reader who, in the last 24 hours, performed an act of kindness — large or small — for a stranger. Give examples to inspire others.

- Shelter a friend? You can if you leave an extra umbrella at work. Then, when the day turns wet, you have some shelter for your umbrella-less friends.
My co-worker Carolyn buys cheap umbrellas. On sale, they're just a couple of bucks. She keeps them at home, in the car, and at work: handy for when a friend needs an umbrella but doesn't need the hassle of trying to remember to return it.
My friend Alex says, "You meet the nicest people under umbrellas in the rain." He uses an extra-large one and when he comes upon a wet soul who forgot his or hers and is going in his direction, he doesn't ask. He just walks up and shares his.

GUERRILLA TIP

Slow down.

By slowing the pace at which we move through the day, we'll give ourselves a better chance to notice and respond to opportunities for the encouraging word or charitable act that can make someone else's day. One of the most popular excuses people give for NOT stopping to help others in need is "I don't have time now." That's why many Kindness Guerrillas choose to not live life in the Fast Lane. We may be in the Last Lane in the competition to acquire personal fortunes, but our jobs and simple lifestyles reflect our priorities: they give us time to respond to others in need.

GUERRILLA TIP

Assume your help is needed.

In ambiguous situations when we're not sure our help is needed, our impulses to act are inhibited by the fear of appearing foolish.

Trust your intuition in such cases. You'll find that your hunches are usually right: people who seem troubled almost always are troubled.

But even when others don't need your help, your offer will be appreciated. In fact, your gift of sensitivity and goodwill — your willingness to help a stranger — may have a far greater impact than whatever it was you volunteered to do!

> *Give what you have. To someone it may be better than you dare to think.*
>
> — Henry Wadsworth Longfellow

• Margaret is a stock broker and knows what working in a pressure-cooker environment is like. She recommends giving a friend who's under a lot of stress a certificate for a professional massage at an athletic club or wellness center.

• One of my kids' favorites: In parking lots, when you see someone finish loading a car, offer to take the shopping cart back into the store. Bonus: Empty shopping carts can be accelerated rapidly; once they're up to warp speed, the captain can hop on for a ride! (Watch out for alien vessels crossing your path.)

• If you're taking a trip in your car, take along a half dozen pre-stamped greeting cards addressed to friends back home. Type the message: "I'm glad you're in the world. A secret admirer." When you stop at truck stops, find drivers who are heading where you're not, and ask them to mail the cards when they've reached their destinations. Explain why you're doing this, and show the driver the cards before you seal them so they'll know your intentions are on the up and up.

Philip and Mary play the same game without leaving town at all. They go to the local Hen House Truck Stop and recruit drivers to mail their greetings from points all over the map!

• A true Kindness Guerrilla, Mike had a wonderful idea: stick a $1 bill on a bulletin board, and attach a note: "Found extra $1 in my pocket. If you need this, please take it." Many people will pass by several times, try to act casual, look suspiciously all around them (looking for the Candid Camera?), and then *not take the money!*

HOW YOU CAN BE KINDER...RIGHT NOW!

We don't need to change ourselves to be kinder. We need change only what we say to ourselves. The kindest among us are those who act in spite of the fearful and meanspirited voices all of us hear.

— Gavin Whitsett

Why don't we behave as kindly as we want to? The chief reason is that we talk ourselves out of acting kindly. Opportunities to do kind deeds and say kind words are lost when we remind ourselves of all the reasons why we shouldn't help others: "I don't want to help out now because _____" (fill in the blank), we say to ourselves. We inhibit our kind behavior by drowning out our kind impulses with negative self-statements.

You can immediately start to be the kindhearted person you want to be by saying positive things to yourself to counter the negative voices. Some of the most common excuses people give themselves for behaving uncharitably are listed in the column on the left. When you find you are restraining a kind impulse, substitute the positive self-statement on the right for the inhibiting thought on the left.

It's inconvenient.	Being kind is more important to me in the long run than many of the usual things that make up my daily routine.
Someone else will help out.	This is my opportunity to demonstrate to myself that I'm the kind of person I want to be.
People will think I'm a nut.	Let people think what they will. I have plenty of friends who admire my efforts to be kind. I don't need everyone's approval.
Others may think I'm a fool.	There are millions of people in the world, thank goodness, who share their resources with others. I don't think they're fools.

I'll scare people.

I'll just walk away quickly after I've done my kind deed so it will be clear that I expect nothing in return.

People will reject me.

People's behavior says more about them than about me. And after all, it was my gift that was rejected. Not me.

It's not going to make any difference.

Treating others with kindness makes me feel good. It's evidence that I'm a person whom I can be proud of being. Plus, kind acts often start chain reactions of kindliness among both recipients and, even, those who merely witness a kindness.

I'm not positive they need my help.

True, but the gesture often means as much as the gift.

The good news is that all of us have kind impulses — those familiar urges to help when we see someone in need. But as Mary Webb points out, "If you stop to be kind, you must swerve often from your path." Kindness Guerrillas have made commitments to themselves to not follow the conventional path, to challenge the customary ways of thinking, and to make the extra effort to yield to those familiar impulses. For all of us that means refuting the world's taken-for-granted cautions — sensible hesitations you might call them — that we absorbed growing up in this society.

The chief obstacle to becoming the person you want to be is inside you; that's where the real kindness revolution is taking place.

> *The improvement of society does not call for any essential change in human nature, but, chiefly, for a larger and higher appreciation of its familiar impulses.*
> — Charles Horton Cooley

GUERRILLA WORKS

- Lottery tickets can be great Guerrilla Kindness fun. Stick some $1 lottery tickets in your wallet or billfold, and leave them for servers who've been helpful or who've seemed especially stressed out.

- Instant-Win Lottery tickets express your appreciation for daily services too. Include one in a monthly payment to your paper delivery person. Or put a ticket in an envelope clipped to your mailbox and addressed to "Mr/Ms Mail Carrier." Enclose a note. An appropriate greeting for both newspaper and mail persons may be, "Hope this is good news for you. Thanks for your great service."

- You can also enjoy the fun of putting mystery in someone's life. Each day for a week, anonymously mail a $1 lottery ticket to a favorite neighbor, teacher, co-worker, or friend. A random kindness option: drop a ticket in another shopper's cart when she's not looking.

• Some years ago scientists found out that plants respond to the moods of the people around them. If there are trees, shrubs, indoor or outdoor plants that have delighted you, take a moment now and then to tell them.

• My friend Maggie lives in a purple house, celebrates Summer Solstice, and hugs her trees. I like that in a friend.

• If you park in the same lot everyday, surprise the attendant! An out-of-the-blue gift of doughnuts, cookies, or candy will make both of you feel good. And a "Thanks for looking out for my car so well, Ed" will make the after-glow even warmer.

• Do you get nervous when others are driving? I do. It's embarrassing that I keep slamming my brake foot on the floor. I can't help it. I also have no control over my hands; they turn blue-white as I stiff-arm the dashboard.
Recognize that passengers in your car are more concerned about speed and possible dangers than when they're behind the wheel. Drive extra slowly and with more distance between yourself and the car ahead than you normally allow.

• When hugging or holding hands with someone, *don't be the first to let go.*

GUERRILLA TIP

Pause... enjoy the high.

Most people notice that doing kind deeds and saying kind words feels good. Researcher Paul Pearsall presents evidence that when we help others, our brains release endorphins, a morphine-like substance that produces feelings of exhilaration — as in the "runners' high." At the same time, our bodies produce other chemicals that inhibit the release of Substance P, the transmitter that communicates pain messages to the brain.

We miss the pleasure unless we pause after performing our kindness, reflect on the experience, and enjoy the brain chemistry... a natural high.

• Be a gentlefriend. On a crowded bus or subway, offer your seat to any fellow passengers who are elderly, have their arms full of packages, or have children with them.

• "Guess what I heard about you, Gavin," says my friend Gary. He believes in Second Hand Praise: passing on to people the positive remarks others have made about them. I'm glad he does. It's a delight to learn that others are so fond of us that we've been the focus of their conversations.

• Secret Signals are a fun way to send personal messages in public. Used to communicate encouragement and affection, Secret Signals can be a hand squeeze, a tug on the ear lobe, a nose scratch, or any other nonverbal sign you work out with your child or special other.
Mamacita, my grandmother, would tap the side of her nose when we were in public. That meant, "I love you." Public outings became fun times to trade secret messages. No one but Mamacita and I knew our secret signal. For me, sharing that Secret Signal was an important part of the bond I felt with Mamacita.

GUERRILLA TIP

Be enthusiastic.

Enthusiasm has a multiplier effect on any kindness. Not surprising really. Many times when we need help we feel timid about asking others to go out of their way for us. What a joy when others respond with a broad smile and hearty, "Happy to help!"

Give, but give joyously, and joy becomes part of the gift.

> *There are persons so radiant, so genial, so kind, so*
> *pleasure bearing, that you instinctively feel in their*
> *presence that they do you good; whose coming into the room*
> *is like the bringing of a lamp there.*
>
> — Henry Ward Beecher

• You'll never fail to put smiles on strangers' faces if you GO B-U-B-B-L-E !!! Take bubbles to the park, beach, or outdoor festivals. Once you start blowing bubbles, kids will want to blow some too, so take extra bottles with you.

For truly awesome bubbles, get *The Unbelievable Bubble Book* by John Cassidy ($9.95 by Klutz Press). It comes with the equipment and simple instructions you need to blow twelve-foot bubbles!

• Dete is the station manager at our public radio station, WNIN-FM. She not only runs a great station, she also makes staff meetings more fun by putting "Hero Of The Week" at the top of the agenda. She picks a different staffer each week, acknowledges a specific good thing the person has done over the last week, and gives him or her the Hero award to keep on display for seven days, until the next meeting.

Dete uses a huggable Pooh Bear, but awards can be trophies, giant blue ribbons, or whimsical toys. Make a big deal out of it by leading the group in a round of applause for each week's Hero.

• Silence is painful sometimes. Especially if you've made a comment and the other person doesn't acknowledge your comment. The silence is frequently interpreted as "I'm not interested in you" or "I'm mad at you."

Dr. Joe Stearns, who taught the first course in Interpersonal Communication I ever took, showed me a neat way of ensuring I acknowledged others. He said "You can develop the habit of verbally responding to others' comments if you'll think of it as completing the loop."

The loop has three parts:

1. PERSON A makes a statement.
2. PERSON B acknowledges the statement.
3. PERSON A confirms the acknowledgment.

The examples below illustrate how you can give people the courtesy of completing the loop.

1. TED: "I saw Suzanne today."
2. ELLIE: "How is she doing?"
3. TED: "She sounds as if she's doing really great."

or

1. BARBARA: "You haven't spoken much tonight."
2. ALEC: "Sorry. Just tired I guess."
3. BARBARA: "Yes, you've had a long day."

• Hate Mondays? Make them Surprise Days. You'll find that you (and the people around you) will start looking forward to Mondays if you make it a habit of surprising others with small delights to start the week off. My friend Jean surprises her co-workers with mints, gum, doughnuts, cookies, or — the favorite of all — fudge brownies with pecans.

• Ask "Do you have a few minutes now?" or "Is this a good time to talk?" when a person answers your telephone call.

• Buy at least $25 worth of greeting cards — birthday cards, sympathy cards, congratulations cards, I-miss-you cards, get well cards, anniversary cards and blank cards — so that you'll always have the right card to send someone you care for, whatever the circumstance, as soon as you get news of the occasion! Keep a roll of stamps handy.

Kathy gave me the idea of keeping a variety of cards at the office too. I had felt so helpless when I would hear of someone's good or bad news when I was at work; now I can have a card on its way in minutes.

GUERRILLA TIP

Discover your personal 20%.

The 80/20 rule was developed by marketing researchers who discovered that 80% of most companies' profits came from 20% of their customers.

The 80/20 rule applies also to the rewards you receive from behaving kindly: 20% of the different kindnesses you perform will account for 80% of the satisfaction you obtain as a Kindness Guerrilla. Identify that fruitful 20% so you can channel your energy into the actions which are most likely to keep you behaving kindly. Although you may occasionally practice all the suggestions in *Guerrilla Kindness*, discover which particular ones are most effective in keeping you motivated and make them a regular part of your Guerrilla Campaign.

• Play hard. Play fair. Nobody hurt. Those are the only groundrules for non-competitive games, one of the most powerful community builders you'll find. The games are family fun, can be played by 2 to 200 participants, are easy to learn, and require little or no equipment. Games are a surefire way to bring folks in a neighborhood together to get acquainted, to laugh, and to enjoy each other.

Recruit a handful of friends to organize a Neighborhood Games Day. You'll find that (1) you can get loads of free publicity for the event from the press, (2) local businesses will donate refreshments, and (3) you'll unleash a flood of goodwill among former strangers.

I organized my first "New Games Day" in Carbondale, Illinois, and it remains one of my most treasured memories of fun and fellowship. I was amazed at how easy it was to put together.

Two books tell you how to build a sense of community in your school, organization, business or neighborhood with cooperative games: *Playfair: Everybody's Guide to Non-Competitive Play,* by Drs. Matt Weinstein and Joel Goodman ($10.95 from Impact Publishers), and *The New Games Book,* edited by Andrew Fluegelman ($12.95 from Doubleday).

GUERRILLA TIP

Surround yourself with reminders.

Most people want to be kind. When you behave unkindly, it's probably because you temporarily forgot how important kindness is to you. That's why it's helpful to have lots of reminders around you wherever you go. (Maybe our "gorilla" can help you remember?)

Keep an inspirational book handy. Wear a piece of jewelry or clothing that reminds you to treat others kindly. Put a poster on your wall. And post little messages at work and in your car that will reduce the chance of your forgetting to be kind.

Here's an angel's reminder:

> *"Go break to the needy sweet charity's bread;*
> *For giving is living," the angel said.*
> *"And must I be giving again and again?"*
> *My peevish and pitiless answer ran.*
> *"Oh no," said the angel, piercing me through,*
> *"Just give til the Master stops giving to you."*

— anonymous

• Birthdays are especially meaningful among the dozen or so close friends that make up my "extended family." One ritual we've established as part of the celebration is that each friend recounts a special kindness or gift they've received from the Birthday Boy or Girl during the past year. It's our way to tell our honored friends not only that we love them, but — through reciting the wonderful things they've done for us — why they are so special to us.

• My students April and Todd take Guerrilla Kindness to the streets. They leave quarters in soda and candy machines along with stick-on notes: "Have one on us...and pass it on! The Kindness Guerrillas."

• Use Third Party Praise. Say positive things about people behind their backs. When the words get back to them — and they usually will — they'll have a greater impact than if delivered directly. The compliment seems much more genuine, and all of us are proud to have other people think so highly of us that we have become the subject of others' conversations.

• Give life. Consider donating blood and signing the organ donor certificate on your driver's license.

• Remember when you went out door-to-door selling peanuts or candy to help your school band buy uniforms? I don't remember the faces to which I made my pitches, but I'll never forget the gratitude I felt for those kind souls who had no earthly use for peanuts in the shell... and yet bought several packages. Even at the time, I was aware that the real message was, "We consider you to be important enough to shell out a dollar or two so you can feel good about yourself." And I did feel good about myself.

Now when I open the door and there is a child with a heavy box of goodies to sell, I know that the purchase I'm being invited to make isn't just about helping charitable groups. It isn't about whether I want to have a pound of chocolate and almonds sitting in my kitchen. The real business is making a good memory of "stranger kindness" for those who are still putting together a view of the world, of strangers, and of themselves.

That's why I encourage you to buy whatever neighborhood children are selling to support a non-profit group project... even if you have no urgent need for mixed nuts in a decorative can.

• Consider leaving your body to a regional medical school. Contact the school, and tell your physician and family about your wishes.

• Use Public Praise. Because it feels so good to be complimented in front of others, use small gatherings as opportunities to say something positive about one of the people in the group.

• When I was young, I would get irritated with senior citizens — "They just move too slowly!" Then I went shopping with Papa, my grandfather, and things changed.
   I was rejoining him after I had gone to another area of the mall, when I made a discovery that forever changed my view of the elderly. Seen from afar, Papa looked exactly like the old people at whom I had so often muttered in impatience. The thought of someone being curt with Papa just because he was slow moving made me sad. Treat the elderly as you wish others would treat your own grandparents.

• Be courteous to telephone sales people, but if you don't want what they're selling tell them right away. If they're reluctant to take "no" for an answer, remain courteous but use the Broken Record Routine. After everything they say, repeat the words "Thanks, but I'm really not interested." Regardless of what they say, keep repeating those same words until they give up. (Tip: *Do not try this at home or with friends you want to keep!*)

THE REMARKABLE HEALTH BENEFITS OF BEING KINDHEARTED

*It is one of the beautiful compensations of this life that
no one can sincerely try to help another without helping
himself.*

— Charles Dudley Warner

In the 1929 classic, *Magnificent Obsession* by Lloyd Douglas, the hero breaks a code and discovers a magnificent secret: astounding benefits will come to anyone who does a good deed for another.

Now there is scientific support for the notion that kind deeds do produce benefits for those people who regularly practice the "magnificent obsession." Allan Luks, in *The Healing Power of Doing Good* has assembled massive medical data that suggest the helping produces benefits for helpers, benefits surprisingly like those we enjoy when we exercise.

Luks and his co-author Peggy Payne present evidence that helping yields many positive psychological and physiological changes:

PSYCHOLOGICAL	PHYSIOLOGICAL
exhilaration	increased body warmth
sense of euphoria	stronger immune system
more energy	reduction of pain
sense of calmness	improved weight control
relaxation	reduced sleeplessness
generally happier	slower progress of cancer
optimism	improved cardiovascular
heightened sense of	reduced acid stomach
well-being	reduced coronary disease
decreased loneliness	drop in blood pressure
decreased hostility	decreased oxygen
decreased depression	consumption
decreased feelings of helplessness	quicker recovery from surgery
feeling healthy	fewer colds
sense of connectedness	better circulation
with others and	relief from arthritis
reminders of our	relief from lupus
membership in some	relief from asthma
larger, spiritual body	greater longevity

In the new field of psychoneuroimmuniology, medical researchers have discovered that kind words and kind deeds help us to stay healthy. Even kind thoughts and feelings of kinship enhance the body's immune system, our first line of defense. Our immunological resistance to the common cold, for example, is significantly increased when we regularly try to help others.

> *We cannot live for ourselves. A thousand fibers connect us with our fellow men; and among those fibers, those sympathetic threads, our actions run as causes, and they come back to us as effects.*
>
> — Hermann Melville

GUERRILLA WORKS

• Spread the good news! Write an article about opportunities for kindness in your area. Make it upbeat and fun, and submit it for publication in a local magazine.

While I wrote this book, I wrote several articles for area newspapers and magazines. I discovered that editors are interested in reading articles that suggest simple, inventive ways to help others. Practical guides to kindness are rare.

• Send flowers to your partner at his or her workplace. When co-workers ask what the occasion is, your mate will have the pleasure of saying, "No special occasion. Just because he/she loves me."

Ask your mate what other cherishing behaviors make him or her feel loved and DO THEM FREQUENTLY. For a thousand more ideas, Gregory Godek's *1001 Ways To Be Romantic* ($10.95, Casablanca Press) is a rich source of fuel to feed the flame in your relationship.

- Resist the urge to be rude back to those who treat you rudely. John, a management consultant, explains it this way. Most people know when they've behaved badly and don't like seeing themselves that way. They are more likely to try to change their behavior if we model a kind response. If, on the other hand, we react discourteously, they will use our rudeness to justify their own. We jeopardize the chance others will learn from their mistakes when we point those mistakes out to them.

- Get a bunch of gift certificates from the best ice cream store in town. Keep them in your desk at work for when you discover its somebody's birthday or other special occasion. Leave them in the person's mailbox, desk, or work station. If you also have a stash of various greeting cards at work, all the better.

- Clergymen and women almost always know of individuals who are struggling through particularly difficult periods of life. But most clergy don't have the time personally to attend to everyone who needs some care. Ask your pastor or rabbi how you can help, and you're sure to find at least one troubled soul to whom your loving attention could bring hope and comfort.

GUERRILLA TIP

Pace yourself for the long haul.

It's unhealthy to take on the burden of having always to do kind deeds for every needy person. When we act because we should rather than because we want to, the burden becomes physically and emotionally draining. The result may be to abandon the kindness campaign altogether.

Even the saints recognized the need to occasionally retreat, gather strength, and renew enthusiasm. Practice saying "No." Regularly take days or even weeks off. Remind yourself that to last for the long haul you'll need to take a break before your career as a Kindness Guerrilla loses its playfulness.

- When paying for your gas, look to see if any cars with out-of-state plates have pulled up for gas. If they have, give the cashier an extra dollar to pay part of their tab. Ask her to say "Welcome to our state."

The first time I tried this, I was able to overhear a young father share his delight with his family as he climbed into the car for which I had bought some gas. "Guess what happened," I heard him say. That was enough to hook me on this particular act of Guerrilla Kindness.

- Become a Good News Reporter. Call the Features Editor of your local newspaper when you hear of exceptional kindnesses performed by individuals or groups in your community.

- Criticize the behavior not the behaver. That is, complain about the performance — what they did or failed to do — instead of the personality, character, attitude, or intention. When you must criticize another, deliver your comments in private.

GUERRILLA TIP

"Stop while you're hot."

That was Ernest Hemingway's advice. Whenever you can, end your day's kindness campaign after an especially positive experience rather than after a kindness that flopped. It's much easier to resume your campaign the next day while you're still enjoying the after-glow of the previous day's success.

You can ensure that your days will end with a glow if every night you spend a moment to make up a list of kind things you can do the next day: calling a friend; complimenting someone on something she did in the last month; repeating your thanks for a friend's or co-worker's help; or writing a loving note you can hide so your mate or child will find it when he's at work or home or school.

• Houseplants are wonderful gifts for home or office. Many live for years and become like members of the family. A houseplant is one gift that doesn't end up in a rummage sale or the back of a drawer. The only problem is that many people don't have the know-how or discipline to keep plants alive. My mother's friend Libby has solved the problem. She gives only six kinds of plants away; all six thrive on abuse.

FOR THE HORTICULTURALLY HAPLESS — those with good intentions but consistent records of bad luck with plants — Libby gives plants that like some light and water but are willing to negotiate about how much:

* The *Spider Plant* (airplane plant) spouts babies in mid-air. It's the most fussy of the three about light and water, but it will still do great in shade and survive occasional forgetfulness about watering. Pest-free and fast growing, the spider plant can live ages in just a glass of water.

* *English Ivy* climbs in sun or darkness and is also forgiving when water is forgotten. The leaves mutate into fascinating shapes and colors.

* *Philodendron* (monstera) lives up to its formal name. This nearly indestructible plant grows to monster proportions: its huge leaves can spread to fill a six- to eight-foot circle.

FOR THE HORTICULTURALLY HOPELESS — those with zero ability to keep even plastic plants pretty — Libby's choices are plants that are indifferent to how much light and water they receive, water-when-you-rememember plants that can live in dark corners:

* The *Madagascara Dragon Tree* (dracaena) grows straight up or in fascinating angles and curves.

* *Pothos* (devil's ivy) grows in long vines that can be draped over doors, windows, mantles, or furniture.

* The *Mother-In-Law's Tongue* (snake plant) is truly indestructible.

- Big impact. Little effort. Volunteer to drive elderly friends on an outing of some sort: shopping, eating out, attending a concert, or just seeing the sights.

Many older people have seen all their closest friends die. Combined with the loss of the ability to drive safely, senior citizens' loneliness becomes an aching isolation. Make a decision to try this just once... a 30 minute drive to see the fall colors, for example... and you'll be awed by your ability to make such a positive impact with so little effort.

- A smart move if you have a friend in a management position: give him or her *Smart Moves* by Sam Deep and Lyle Sussman ($7.95, Addison-Wesley). Your friend will find over 1,600 tips ranging from how to keep a boss happy, what to do if your boss is a jerk, how to start meetings on time, and how to remember others' names... to how to sell your ideas to others and how to instill pride in your employees.

GUERRILLA TIP

Avoid negative people.

Cynical people can drag everyone around them into their dark space. I feel embarrassed about my enthusiasm and faith in humanity when I'm around negative people. By scheduling weekly lunch dates with friends who share my delight in surprising strangers with kindness, I'm able to sustain my optimism and high energy level. Try to work in regular visits with positive people and give wide berth to the cynics.

> *New and stirring ideas are belittled because if they are*
> *not belittled the humiliating questions arises, "Why then*
> *are you not taking part in them?"*
>
> — H. G. Wells

• I asked my little sister if she thought children should have their own space that parents enter only when invited. Becky, who has four kids — from 10 to 16 — asked, "Do you mean physical space or metaphysical space?" I settled back for a long discussion. It was obvious my sister had given this question some thought.

The conclusion was that children should have both: not only a room or area of a room that is private, but also the freedom to feel and think as they wish, to have secrets, and to know that all areas of their privacy will be respected.

• Return anything you borrow in better shape than when you received it. Clean it, fill it with gas, sharpen it, and so forth. My friend Ellen also includes a note and a handful of Hershey's Kisses when she returns borrowed items. "Sweets to the sweet," she writes.

• If friends are hit with some sort of crisis that will reduce the time and energy they have to prepare meals, make a casserole, lasagna, or pot of stew they can throw in the microwave and eat on the run.

Nana keeps frozen lasagna in microwave-safe containers. As soon as she hears of another's need, she drops off one of the containers.

• Play Treasure Hunt at the library. Put half a $1 bill into a book that doesn't get checked out often. Include a note that says "Congratulations, Treasure Hunter." Return it to the shelf. Put the other half of the bill into a popular magazine in the reading room along with a mysterious note giving instructions where the other half can be found.

The adventure is more fun if you hang around to see the action. A variation: Use a $5 bill and put instructions in a chain of books that ultimately lead to the treasure.

• Keep a sharp eye out for any opportunity to help your neighbors — move a new refrigerator in, take down a tree, or tackle some other Herculean task. If you wait until you're asked to help, you've waited too long.

• Mister Viol, my 5th grade math teacher, told us that character is how a person behaves when nobody is watching. If you dent or scratch a parked car, leave your name and phone number on the windshield of the damaged car.

GUERRILLA TIP

Practice smiling.

You can actually make your smile brighter and more natural by practicing your smile in private. Stretch your face into as broad a smile as possible, hold the smile muscles tense for 15 seconds, and then let go.

This isometric exercise of the *zygomaticus major* — the main smile muscle — relaxes the lower face and jaw. That's one of the places where a lot of us carry around our worries.

Yes, it sounds silly, but try it. You'll find your face naturally assumes a comfortable, easy smile. Further, if you practice in your car, you'll have given the gift of amusement to anyone who happens to see you!

• A wonderful memory. On the hottest summer days, Mr. Winslow would put his sprinkler on the sidewalk in front of his house. We neighbor kids quickly sensed the opportunity for fun.

• People with foreign accents like to be noticed. Ask them to tell you about their homeland. Begin a friendly exchange with something simple like "Hi, my name is Gavin. I was wondering where you're from."

• The Guerrilla Kindness revolution began when strangers started caring for one another's cars. Without recognition or reward, the first Kindness Guerrillas began putting money into others' expired parking meters, turning off the lights of empty cars in parking lots, rolling up the windows of vacant cars when it was raining, and picking up and paying others' parking tickets. Kindness Guerrillas are still caring for strangers by caring for strangers' cars.

GUERRILLA TIP

Say "yes" to the child within.

Taking a playful attitude will inspire some of your most delightful Guerrilla Works. Assert your right to be silly and frivolous, give in to that interior Frisky Kid that the Act-Your-Age-Police would have you sit on, and you can develop capers that will get even the grown-ups smiling.

> *When in doubt, make a fool of yourself. There is a microscopically thin line between brilliantly creative and acting like the most gigantic idiot on earth. So what the hell, leap.*
>
> — Cynthia Heimel

• Take the attitude that one of the people you talk with on Fridays is going to die at midnight. You don't know who. Extend special courtesy to everyone and show them all the kindness you would if they had only hours to live.

• My sister Nan arranged for a surprise conference call for my parents' 50th anniversary. There were eight of us on the phone talking about how special my folks are.

Conference calls are great fun for all happy occasions. Your long distance company will tell you how to set one up. All you need to do is contact friends or family to be included, set up a convenient time for the call, tell the phone company when you want to place the call, and make sure the recipients of your kind gesture will be by the phone.

• Encourage your teenagers to interview their grandparents. All will feel much closer after the experience. Suggest questions that will lead the grandparents to talk about their lives and family history.

• When you see a couple or small group taking photographs of one another, volunteer to take a photo of the whole group.

KINDNESS GUERRILLAS STRUT THEIR STUFF

A great man shows his greatness by the way he treats little men.

— Thomas Carlyle

The front rank. They wield enormous economic and political power. And there are 69 million of them in America. They're the Baby Boomers, now early 30s to early 50s, and they are defining this decade in a way that's taken social scientists by surprise. After gorging themselves on money and things in the 80's, they've become America's most spiritually absorbed generation in the 90's.

Demographic researcher Brad Edmondson concludes his latest study of the Boomers with the observation that this generation is now putting less emphasis on money and more on basic values. Increasingly, Boomers are responding to *Rolling Stone's* call to "muster the will to remake ourselves into altruists...."

Good Housekeeping, in a special ad in *The New York Times,* welcomes America to the 90's, "the Decency Decade, the year the good guys finally win..." and urges readers to "live healthier, more decent lives."

Neil Howe and William Strauss, authors of *Generations: The History Of America's Future,* write that Boomers are "obsessed with values, back-to-basics movements," and, in a "recent turn away from yuppie-style consumption," are "determined to reinfuse the entire society with meaning" and compassion. In the December '92 *Atlantic,* Howe and Strauss sum up what appears to be the new ethic of America's most powerful population; it is the conviction that "Life's smallest acts exalt (or diminish) one's personal virtue."

In 1988 President George Bush called for "a kinder, gentler nation" and urged Americans to join his "1000 Points of Light." The next generation of leaders to take the reins seem determined to actualize the promise of President Bush's vision. Guerrilla Kindness has become respectable. Even legitimate. But the important test is to see if we really can shake off materialistic obsession and live lives that affirm the innate goodness and charity of our species. Now we have the political power to do it.

> *There is a slow movement in history towards the recognition of a man by his fellow man. When this happens, all that has been done in the past will fall into place and find its true value.*
>
> — Jean-Paul Sartre

GUERRILLA WORKS

- My doctor gave me a pamphlet about how to fit exercise into one's daily routine. The suggestion to "take the most remote parking spot" in a large lot appealed to me because it would leave the nearer spots for those who really need them — the elderly, parents with young children, those in a hurry, and others who don't need the exercise you and I need.

- Biff and Ann are busy professionals but they make a point every two months to drop off their old magazines at the county jail. It takes less than 30 minutes, and it's a kindness that would be appreciated also at many other places: laundromats, waiting rooms, the hair stylist, the fitness center, and such.

- Kathy loves it when friends clip articles, pictures, cartoons, poems, and other information they think she might enjoy and send them with a simple "Thought you might like this." That's how she discovered *The Utne Reader, The Atlantic,* and *Parabola.*

- Make someone's day for the price of a couple of stamps and ten minutes of your time. Drop a note to your child's favorite teacher, the principal, the school board — or all three. Let them know that your child likes and respects his or her teacher, and thank them for helping raise your child to be a competent, thoughtful, and informed adult.

• Organize a Mall Marathon. With three other members of your guerrilla group, saturate a mall with kindness. A pair of Kindness Guerrillas begins at opposite ends of a mall; within each pair, one person takes the left lane of the walkway, the other takes the right.

At a set time, all of you begin walking to the opposite ends of the mall. Each of you smiles, says "Hi," and delivers a simple compliment to as many people as you can. Compliments might focus on others' appearance, apparel, behavior, or youngsters-in-tow.

Variations: (a) Do the Mall Marathon by yourself. (b) Don't try to include compliments; just smile and say "Hi." Or (c) address only senior citizens; only people of the same gender; only people by themselves; or only people who look tired, sad, or in a bad mood.

- Hatefulness is not the opposite of kindness. Indifference is.

The father of modern psychology, William James, declared that the most basic needs are the needs to feel noticed and appreciated. We can make others feel good about themselves — and us! — by SOFTENing them up when they're talking to us.

SOFTEN is an acronym for 6 behaviors which communicate to others that we're interested and listening to them:

S Smile.

O Open posture: keep your arms and legs uncrossed and turn your body to directly face the other.

F Forward lean: lean toward the other so that your head is no more than an arm's length away.

T Touch: shake hands at meeting and parting and look for appropriate moments to touch the other's upper arm lightly and briefly.

E Eye contact. It's the single most important nonverbal message system in communicating interest and warmth.

N Nodding your head and saying "uh-huh" in response to what the other is saying.

- Be the first to make eye contact, smile, and say "Hi" to strangers. What a joy to see even the most dour, somber faces slip into smiles.

- A friend I admired in graduate school responded to compliments with, "Thanks, that makes me feel good." I had always bumbled around when I was complimented. Frequently I wound up discounting the action or feature on which I was being complimented. The end result of such a discounting response was that the kindness of the person complimenting me was discounted.

  Now I know how to acknowledge others' generous words. It's honest… it's easy… and it allows them to enjoy the after-glow of being kind. Just "Thanks, that makes me feel good!"

- Cheryl believes it's a first principle of courtesy. if you're going to be late, let others know.

- When you hear of someone giving up smoking, beginning a diet, starting to exercise regularly, returning to school to get a degree, or becoming a volunteer with some non-profit group, write him or her a "Way-To-Go!" note.

GUERRILLA TIP

Don't expect appreciation.

Many people don't know how to respond to an unexpected kindness. Others... because of their own hidden agendas... won't. When you do see the surprised smile or hear the genuine "thank you," it will be all the sweeter.

Remind yourself that you are the one who has made a commitment to be kind; not the other fellow. And you are the one who is gaining the satisfaction of seeing your own goodness come to light.

> *He who praises another enriches himself far more than he does the one praised. To praise is an investment in happiness.... The poorest human being has something to give that the richest could not buy.*
>
> — George Matthews Adams

• How can you make compliments more believable? In a society where kind words are so often phony, it's a real concern.

When you compliment others, *be as specific as possible.* Give the details and examples of what they did that pleases you. "You're terrific" comes straight from the bag of generic compliments. Compare it to "I like the way you always ask how others are getting along and then really listen to what they have to say — as you did this morning with Karen."

• When you read an article about local people doing something positive, drop Way-To-Go notes in the mail to them and enclose the clippings you read. My Dad has done this for years and made lasting correspondents along the way.

• When you read about some tragedy involving local people, write them a sympathy note even if you don't know them. Notes can be as simple as "Dear Friends, Although we're not acquainted, I wanted to express my sympathy for your recent loss. I know this must be a very difficult time for you. I wish you peace and hope and happier days."

If you can't find the addresses in your phone book, call the reporters who wrote the stories.

- Resist the urge to give advice. As the saying goes "Wise people don't need it, and fools won't heed it." Plus, advising others about what to do obliges them to later defend their decision if they choose to not follow our advice.

You can help others tap into their own wisdom by asking questions such as,

* "Why is this a problem for you?"
* "How do you hope the situation will turn out?"
* "What's your most important priority in this situation?
* "How would you advise me if I had that problem?"
* "What is it that you most want to avoid happening in this situation?"
* "What would make you feel best about yourself?"
* "What do you think would be the best decision for everybody involved, in the long run?"

- Two very large limbs lay in my backyard for months. I didn't want to rent a chain saw to cut up just two limbs, but Jason, who lives right behind us, came over one afternoon. "I rented this chain saw, and I've finished using it. Do you want to use it before I take it back?" "Yes, that's just the thing I can use on some downed limbs I have," I said. If you rent a piece of equipment — post hole digger, chain saw, lawn de-thatcher, etc. — ask a neighbor if he or she would like to use it before you take it back.

• Compound kindness. Wake up one morning and, before you get out of bed, decide to build a Kindness Chain. Once your feet hit the floor, compliment the first ten people you see that day.

Joseph has four daughters so his Kindness Chain is half-finished by the time he walks into his office. The next five people he sees get complimented on something they're wearing, something they're doing, or something they did during the past week.

Patty has a single roommate. She completes her chain with the next nine people she sees in her dorm. Her chain is already done before she walks into the Student Center for breakfast.

If only half of the people in your chain decide to pass their kindnesses on to 10 people they meet that day, and half of those people pass on the kindnesses they received to 10 people, and half of those people... and so on... you may be the proud progenitor of a 3,125 happy hearts by lunch time!

GUERRILLA TIP

Give thanks for the kindnesses you receive.

Try to be aware of every kindness you receive and be specific when you thank the giver.

Many times givers won't even be aware of what they've done; perhaps to them it was just common courtesy. But specifically identifying what the other did and thanking them is a wonderful kindness in itself.

Furthermore, expressing appreciation for a behavior — "reinforcing a behavior" as psychologists say — increases the chance the behavior will be repeated for others. And remember, your kind words will have a longer-lasting effect if you (a) thank the person when others are around, (b) repeat your thanks some days or weeks later, and (c) tell others of your appreciation (frequently your words will get back to the person to whom you're grateful).

• Apologize first. Apologies don't have to be admissions of guilt; they're appropriate whenever any encounter with another has caused hurt. "Even though I was here on time," you might say, "I'm sorry our misunderstanding made you feel forgotten when I didn't show up when you thought I would."

Lots of times, however, you'll find that there was something in what you did that you wish you'd done differently. Apologizing for that will go a long way in reducing the defensiveness and tension created by your exchange.

• The sweetest sound in the world? It's silly maybe, but all of us love to hear our names. My Dad taught me to *use others' names frequently* when talking to them.

Try it. Begin and end conversations on an upbeat by making the first and last word you utter be the other's name. Notice the difference in warmth when you say "It's good to see you" and "John, it's good to see you." There's also a noticeable difference in warmth when you use another's name when you compliment them. Compare "You're a great dancer" and "Tony, you're a great dancer."

- Guerrilla frivolity! When Larry, Beth, and the kids came to visit us last summer, they hid packs of M&Ms all over the house so we would find them after they'd left. It was such fun — Kathy and I were still finding M&Ms months later. (Watch out where you hide them in hot weather!)

- Do you want to soften some of life's hard edges? Keep an eye open as you go through catalogs for things that would make life more comfortable for an elderly friend: scissors that are easy to hold, a calculator with large keys, clocks that flash the time on the ceilings of dark rooms, oversized lamp switches that are easy to grasp, and so forth.

- It's a secret most great hosts have applied for years. When Marion introduces people who don't know one another, she makes it easy for them to talk. By saying a little something about each — job, interests, hometown — she gives them something to talk about!

- Make every day Valentine's Day. Stash packs of children's Valentine's cards in your glove compartment, your desk at work, or in a pocket when you're heading out to do guerrilla work. Leave them so friends, co-workers, and strangers will find them when you're not around. Sign them "from a Secret Admirer," "Cupid Lives" or "Can't wait to Valentine's Day. YOU'RE TOO CUTE!"

• June calls less-mobile friends — friends with babies, shut-ins, and neighbors who are ill — to ask if she can pick something up for them when she's going shopping or to the library or video store. "I call them regularly anyway," she says, "and picking up the few things they need adds only a few minutes to my trip."

• Never miss another's birthday or anniversary again. Go through your yearly calendar and write in reminders five days ahead of special occasions. If you have a personal computer with an alarm/message system, set the system so that reminders will pop up on your screen five days in advance. This will give you time to find a card and get it in the mail.

• In the spring and fall when it's not too hot, buy two or three carnations. As you go about your daily errands, select two or three parked cars and leave a single flower under the windshield wipers of each.

I place carnations and some greenery on cars in the grocery parking lot, for example, and then slyly watch people's reactions. Many times their faces shine with the wonder and pleasure you see on kids' faces on Christmas morning.

GUERRILLA TIP

Attach no strings.

Guerrilla Kindness is revolutionary precisely because it is self-less. That is, we operate on the love motive rather than the profit motive.

There are two guidelines we want to keep in mind. First, practice kind words and kind deeds only with those from whom you don't want anything in return. Second, avoid tit for tat. Don't use your kind gestures to "repay what you owe" another for his or her kindness. Resist the urge, for example, to compliment someone who has just complimented you.

> *Loving kindness is practiced in two ways: first we show kindness to those who have no claim whatever upon us; second, we are kind to those to whom it is due but in a greater measure than is due to them.*
>
> — Maimonides

• Don't be phony when you can't remember another's name. Just say, "Sorry, but I'm having a mental block and can't remember your name." Reminding others of your name is frequently helpful too. If there is the slightest doubt they have forgotten your name, work your name into your casual greeting: "Hi, Dennis. Gavin Whitsett"

• I interviewed Vicki, a child psychologist, for an article I was going to write. She told me that one of the most important gifts parents can give their kids is to set aside five to ten minutes a day — perhaps at supper time — for children to talk about their days. Vicki says it's especially important that youngsters get help in identifying and labeling their feelings.

• Do you grow weary standing in long lines? Imagine how elderly people feel. Let senior citizens in the line ahead of you at busy check-out counters at the post-office, at the library, or in any other line that will require them to stand more than a couple of minutes.

GUERRILLA TIP

Beat your record.

You'll start to notice many more opportunities for Guerrilla Kindness if you keep track of how many you respond to.

Count the number of times you behave in a kindly fashion each day, and then try beat your record. This simple task can have profound results. Students in my classes discover they are much kinder than they had previously thought. And people who start to see themselves as kind start to behave even more kindly. It's a kindness circle that keeps growing!

A handy way to record how many kindnesses you do is to keep a bunch of pennies in your right pocket, then move one to the left pocket each time you perform a Guerrilla Work. At the end of the day, count the pennies in your left pocket.

• Buy several copies of *Rebuilding: When Your Relationship Ends* by Bruce Fisher ($9.95, Impact Publishers). Send them to friends who've broken up with a lover or suffered the loss of a loved one. Write a brief personal note on the front page. Don't mention the book when you see your friend; if the book was useful they'll let you know.

• If someone embarrasses himself in a public place — drops things, stumbles, or knocks things over — immediately go to his aid. As you help him pick-up, say, "I did the same thing once."

• Marion's eyes light up when she finds suggestion or comment boxes. For her, they represent opportunities for acts of Guerrilla Kindness. She first learns staff peoples' names and then writes notes praising the individual workers.

Filling out a comment card takes less than 60 seconds — one of the most effortless kindnesses one can perform — but it's surprising how few people do it. Because they're used so infrequently (and then more often than not used to complain about something), your positive comments carry enough weight to lighten the weight that others carry.

WARM FUZZIES R US

It is the human things that make life good, the unexpected
kindness, the friendly note, the bracing word, the
neighbor's extra loaf of bread she leaves at our back door.
                                        — Raymond J. Baughan

"I don't know why I was so uncomfortable. He was warm and friendly... acted like he was happy to see me... but I left with the feeling he didn't really want me there at all. I guess I'm just being paranoid."

No. You're not. You've just been given a dose of Plastic Fuzzies.

Some years ago Claude Steiner wrote a delightful yarn about Warm Fuzzies, Cold Pricklies, and Plastic Fuzzies. They're the alternate ways we treat one another.

Warm Fuzzies are the currency of Kindness Guerrillas. Including the whole range of kind things we say and do, Warm Fuzzies make people feel noticed, appreciated, and understood.

Once upon a time when Warm Fuzzies were freely traded, a bad witch cast a spell that made folks feel foolish for giving away something for which they got no return. Men and women and children restrained their kindhearted dispositions toward others and began to deliver Cold Pricklies and Plastic Fuzzies.

Cold Pricklies are the mean things we do. They include, as well, indifference and the impersonal ways we treat the anonymous people in our daily passings. And Plastic Fuzzies are the phony affections that compose such a large chunk of "polite" social interaction. The two produce a similar effect: both make people feel bad.

The witch's spell was broken, in Steiner's story, when a Gentle Stranger appeared. Unafraid of being taken advantage of or of appearing foolish, the stranger generously gave out Warm Fuzzies to everyone. Wherever she went, people were enchanted by her radiant goodwill and generosity.

Gradually the men and women and children who had lived under the Witch's yoke began to reclaim their kindliness and to follow the Gentle Stranger's example. A kindness revolution erupted in that unhappy land and soon everyone was acting like Kindness Guerrillas, passing out Warm Fuzzies randomly and even to those who hadn't done anything to earn them.

The story of the Warm Fuzzies, Cold Pricklies, and Plastic Fuzzies helps me understand several facts. One is that in any encounter, how we act does make an impact. And there are few neutral impacts: if we're not delivering a Warm Fuzzy, we're probably shelling out either a Cold Prickly or Plastic Fuzzy.

Another truth is that the Gentle Stranger is the person I want to be. I'm disappointed when I give in to my fear of appearing foolish and to the fear of being taken advantage of. On each person with whom I interact during the day, I want to leave a warm and fuzzy imprint. Steiner's story helps me understand the choices I make every time my life intersects another.

If the world seems cold to you, kindle fires to warm it.
— Lucy Larcom

GUERRILLA WORKS

• As soon as our neighbor Mrs. Durrell learns that new neighbors or co-workers are moving into town, she calls the Chamber of Commerce and has orientation/information packs mailed to the newcomers. Then she pays a brief visit and takes them:

* a loaf of fresh-baked bread,
* a city and state map,
* a city newspaper,
* directions to the nearest grocery, hardware store, and convenience store,
* the phone number for the time and temperature,
* her home and office phone numbers,
* an easy-to-care-for house plant,
* recommendations for a good plumber, electrician, and fix-it outfit.

Why go to the trouble? Mrs. Durrell told me that a stranger had done just such a thing for her when she moved to Evansville many years ago, and the kindness helped her resolve the "Did we do the right thing moving here?" question that most of us face when we make a big change in our lives.

- Wipe out anonymity. You make yourself and others feel more at home in this world when you learn others' names. Eliminating strangerhood is especially warming when you use the names of people in anonymous service jobs: waitresses, maintenance personnel, clerks, and attendants. Remember that everyone wants to be noticed and to feel important!

- Guerrillas can be sweet. Buy dessert for a fellow diner the next time you're out with a group of friends. Ask the waiter or waitress to tell the stranger to pick any treat from the dessert menu and IT'S FREE. Be sure to remain anonymous.

- "Set your things down, why don't you?" she asked while writing her check. Because I was struggling with an armful of merchandise at the checkout while waiting for her, I appreciated the invitation. "Aha," I thought, "a great suggestion for my kindness book." Invite others to lay their purchases on the counter while you pay the cashier. Your kindness will be appreciated.

GUERRILLA TIP

Act the part.

Although we usually think of behavior as being caused by our emotions, the reverse is also true. Drama students who learn Method Acting, for example, discover they can create feelings in themselves just by acting as if they already have them.

In the distinguished journal *Science,* Paul Ekman describes experiments in which subjects were able to create various emotional states just by altering their nonverbal behavior.

Respond to opportunities for small kindnesses when you're feeling cranky and before long you'll start to actually feel kinder.

> *Do not ask me to be kind; just ask me to act as though I were.*

> — Jules Renard

• Take F.I.D.O. with you every time you hop into your car. When someone wrongs you — jumps in front of you in line, pulls out in front of you on the road, or zips into the parking space for which you had patiently waited, for example — remember F.I.D.O.: *Forget It and Drive On!*

• Each Christmas, Cindy and Mike anonymously give a year's AAA membership to an elderly friend who still drives.

• Wave to kids in school buses, folks sitting on their front porches, police officers, firemen, truck drivers, school crossing guards, people in other cars, hot-air balloons, on trains, and on boats.

• Heading west on I-64 in Kansas, I pulled into a truckstop right behind a motorist I had been following for the last 100 miles. We both bee-lined to the Men's Room. When we had finished answering nature's call, I saw him using paper towels to wipe out the sink after he had washed his hands. "Did someone leave a mess," I asked. "No," he replied, "My parents told us kids to always leave public bathrooms cleaner than the way we found them, and now it's a habit with me."

Good habit, I thought.

GUERRILLA TIP

Brainstorm for ideas.

At the top of a blank sheet of paper, write "Kind Things I Would Like Others To Do For Me." Then give yourself five minutes to fill the page with every idea that comes to you, no matter how wacky some may be. If you get stuck, select one of the "things" you've already written and try a free association with that.

Brainstorming works great in groups. And it's a proven way to increase empathy. With your church, school, or scout group, brainstorm for answers to questions such as, "What would I like others to do for me if I were poor (or elderly, or sick, or depressed, or a new guy in town)?"

Brainstorming is a good way to wake up your imagination, click into your right-brain creative powers, and give you ideas for kindnesses others might like from you.

- *Never tell a person he or she is wrong.* If you must give an opposite opinion, acknowledge that the other may be correct but that you have different figures. Then state your view provisionally: "You may be correct about that. I have a somewhat different view, though. I believe...."

- Dan spends time alone once a month with each of his four kids. Each child wants to do something different on the "date," and Dan happily obliges. One month he saw "Rocky Horror Picture Show," attended a two-hour class on origami, watched cars bash each other to bits in a Destruction Derby, and caught 16 blue gill (or one blue gill 16 times).

- Tell your best friends that they're your best friends.

- Sneak in a typed, unsigned note when written assignments are being collected in a class you especially enjoy. Tell the teacher you look forward to coming to his or her class. That note may be the most precious message your teacher has received in months.
The same kind of anonymous warm fuzzy can be slipped into a favorite boss's in-basket.

GUERRILLA TIP

Start a wave of kindness.

Social scientists have proved that people who receive, or even witness simple acts of decency and generosity are themselves stimulated to behave benevolently. The domino effect has been documented in *Cruelty and Kindness,* researcher Harvey Hornstein's review of hundreds of studies. If you slow down or stop your car to let me into the lane ahead of you, for example, I'm much more likely to do the same for another motorist. Know that your kindness campaign does make a difference that makes a difference.

> *How many troubled, crooked, miserable conditions there are*
> *which are just awaiting the arrival of some simple, human*
> *ministry, and they will be immediately transformed!*
> — John Henry Jowett

• My first act as a Kindness Guerrilla... and still one of my favorites: I buy two rolls of LifeSavers along with my other purchases at the grocery. When I'm ready to leave, I give one each to the startled clerk and bagger. It's no wonder I keep doing it when I hear exclamations like "Oh, YOU'RE the candy man. I've heard about you. You gave LifeSavers to Marty last week. She said it made her day."

• Looking for a simple way to feel good about yourself...on even your lowest days? Resolve to *pick up just one piece of litter every time you are out in public.*

• When friends are laid up, Uncle Albert will take them wacky, easy-reading magazines like *The National Lampoon, The National Inquirer* or *Mad Magazine.* CeCe makes a point to call ill friends at least once a day and tell them something amusing she saw or heard that day. When I was home with the flu last winter, friends at work dedicated funny songs to me on my favorite radio station. Laughter is good medicine.

• Ask for help. Give others the pleasure of demonstrating their wisdom, talent, or kindliness.

GUERRILLA TIP

Take the Vacation Perspective.

Ever notice how easy and satisfying it is to treat others warmly and generously when we're on vacation? We seem more willing to adventure, to get to know strangers, and to behave graciously.

Practice taking the Vacation Perspective in your daily life by telling yourself, "I'll only be here once. I may as well as live as fully and lovingly as I can."

It really works. How you see yourself changes how you see others. Seeing yourself as an adventurer and strangers as fellow travelers makes it easier to extend warmth and courtesy even when you're not on vacation.

• On a hot day, buy a six-pack of cold sodas and give it to a road crew or others working outside. On a cold day, pick up several coffees-to-go, lots of cream and sugar, and stirrers and give them to those having to work outside. Be casual; just drive up, hand the things to one of the workers, and drive off in cloud of dust (saying "Hi Ho Silver" or carving a giant "Z" with your sword is optional).

• Social scientists have discovered that when people like one another, they tend to mirror each other's posture and gestures. Most people aren't consciously aware of this mirroring, but when we copy others' nonverbal behaviors — crossing and uncrossing our arms and legs, leaning forward or back, turning our bodies to directly or indirectly face the other, and touching our heads and faces — others get the impression that we like them. Try it. Mirroring is fun to experiment with and, I believe, you'll find that this kindness communicates positive messages... even without the recipient being aware of it.

• Several times a year, Mary Frances drops off a bag of doughnuts at the police and fire stations. "They're the only people I can think of who put their lives on the line every day when they go to work. I just want them to know I'm glad they're there!"

• Use brief, time-limited encounters as opportunities to contribute to global warming. In elevators, waiting rooms, restaurant lounges, and during other stray moments, you can initiate small talk that transforms silent, impersonal minutes into warm, shared moments.

There are three subjects you can easily begin a conversation about: yourself, the other person, or the present situation. And there are three types of statements you can make: state an opinion, disclose a feeling, or ask a question.

An especially effective combination is to (1) make a statement regarding some feature that is puzzling, surprising, or pleasing about the situation, and (2) ask a question related to that feature. For example, "I just noticed there's no one smoking in here. What do you think of that new law against smoking in public buildings?"

Another combination: (1) state an opinion about something the other person is carrying, wearing, or doing, and (2) ask a question. "That's really a clever T-shirt design. Where did you find it?"

• Leave it to Uncle Sam to broadcast your kind and encouraging words from SEE to shining SEE... and beyond. Just write positive messages on the back of the envelopes you mail. Letters pass through many hands, and lots of hearts may be lightened a bit by messages such as "Just like the U.S. Mail, smiles reach the hard to reach places."

• When Alan and Judi are at a bar and see a rather-plain someone sitting alone, they anonymously buy the person a drink. "It's from a secret admirer," the waitress says when she delivers it. Alan and Judi began doing this on their honeymoon, and this particular Guerrilla Work triggers a lot of good memories for them.

• "What's with this guy?" others might wonder. To me it's obvious. Stan — a junior executive with a large accounting firm — is also a Kindness Guerrilla. Not out to make just himself look impressive, Stan always has something positive to say about his co-workers at staff meetings with the boss.

• Aggressively search for opportunities to *catch kids doing something right* — being neat, being kind to animals, sharing, expressing sympathy, or attending to assigned chores. Express your thanks or admiration. Let them know the specific behavior you appreciated.

GUERRILLA TIP

Make kindness a routine.

You're more likely to keep the habit of acting kindly if you can weave kindheartedness into your daily routine: complimenting your co-workers first thing in the day, for example, or expressing your appreciation for the quality of work done by your co-workers; always having a kind word for the waitress who serves you lunch; being a courteous driver; or everyday doing something that communicates your appreciation to your family.

Guerrilla Kindness is not composed of kindness episodes. Our character is defined by the way we live life minute by minute by minute.

> *How easy it is for one benevolent being to diffuse pleasure*
> *around him, and how truly is a kind heart a fountain of*
> *gladness, making everything in its vicinity to freshen into*
> *smiles.*
>
> — Washington Irving

• The dining cars on Amtrak trains are always full, so people share tables. That's where I learned how much fun it is to meet people over a great meal. When restaurants are full and you're alone, offer to share your table or booth with strangers.

• Seized by the rising tide... caving in destruction... sandcastles reclaimed by the sea.
During my last vacation at the ocean, I watched a group of four people build dazzling sand structures. There were towers, shell decorations, and a huge moat surrounding all. Everyday they built their monument to frivolity at low tide so that, after supper, all the other guests at the hotel could gather to watch THE FALL!

• Lifting heavy bags off airport conveyor belts is awkward for anyone, but especially so for the elderly and short folks. Give a hand.

• Popcorn day. Why not? Most offices have microwave ovens for the staff, so you can easily make Fridays Popcorn Day where you work. Bring in a large bowl and several packs of microwave popcorn; pop the corn and let the gang feast all day.

BEASTS IN HARMONY

No lions rage against the lioness;
The tiger to the tigress is not fierce;
No eagles do their fellow birds oppress;
The hawk does not the hawk with talons pierce;
All couples live in love by nature's law....

— William Heale

Beasts have a lot to teach us about kindness, I believe. And about life. Samuel Butler once wrote, "All the animals except man know that the ultimate purpose of life is to enjoy it."

Humankind's closest relative, the great ape, is a particularly good model of gentleness. And the powerful Gorilla, vegetarian and peaceful, is not unusual in the care it takes for its brothers and sisters. Scientists have observed animal altruism in both natural and laboratory settings.

* Pelicans will feed one of their number who has lost its sight and would starve without their help.

* Porpoises protect female porpoises during the birthing process — a time when the mother could not evade sharks — by forming a defensive ring around her.

* Howler monkeys slow down when they're making their way across the forest canopy if one of their group is lame and cannot travel as fast as the others. Being left behind would leave the injured monkey vulnerable to many predators.

* Rhesus monkeys in laboratory experiments refuse to pull the levers that deliver food pellets when they see that pulling the lever will also cause an electrical shock to another monkey.

* Many animals — from robins and thrushes to vervet monkeys — utter a piercing warning cry when a predator approaches. The shriek enables the others of its kind to hide or flee but also attracts the predator's attention, and the sentinel is often killed.

* Wolves will adopt the offspring of other wolves that have been killed.

* Although chimpanzees can't swim and are terrified of water, they will leap into the water if there is a chance they can save another chimpanzee who has fallen in.

Examples of kindness in the non-human animal world support the belief that kindness is a natural element in the human animal world as well.

> *Animals are such agreeable companions. And among them all, only one is ever mean. That one, of course, is us.*
> — anonymous

GUERRILLA WORKS

• Do you wander when a friend is talking to you about something that's important to him or her? Because we think at 600 words per minute but can talk at only about 150 words per minute, it's tough to concentrate on what others are telling us. We have a lot of surplus brain power when we listen.

Harness your attention by using your surplus brain power to *study all of your friend's verbal and nonverbal messages.* As you listen, try to:

* periodically summarize for yourself what your friend has said so far,
* make connections between the various thoughts and feelings your friend has expressed,
* identify what seems to be the most important point to your friend,
* interpret your friend's body language,
* guess about the obvious and not-so-obvious feelings your friend is experiencing, and
* see the "meaning behind the words."

• Slip kind greetings into books you return to the library, magazines on airplanes, menus at restaurants, hymnals at church, and paper tablets wherever school supplies are sold. Try "He who laughs, lasts. Have a great day."

• Some people say that life's greatest gifts are the joys of family life. But families are so fractured these days. Lots of us miss out on the rewards of having children, brothers and sisters, uncles and aunts, and grandparents. Become an Uncle Bob or an Aunt Mary to some friend's child; be a Big Brother or Big Sister; or adopt some grandparents. Big Brothers & Sisters is probably listed in your phone book. To find the nearest Foster Grandparents agency, call the national toll-free number, 1-800-645-3016.

• While in graduate school, Kathy and I adopted Grandma and Grandpa Waller, who owned the farm we lived on. Our relationship with them became as close as our relationships with our natural grandparents. Grandma fed us; Grandpa entertained us with stories. And we gave them our love and assistance in the chores that had become too much for them.

GUERRILLA TIP

Practice in the Comfort Zone.

When launching your career as a Kindness Guerrilla, you may be uncomfortable at first — especially if you're more of an introvert and reaching out to strangers is a new experience for you. Feeling awkward doesn't mean you're doing anything weird or bad; just doing something new. All of us feel awkward when first practicing new skills. You can reduce your discomfort by practicing only where and with whom you feel most comfortable. Start at home. Then include friends. Later move to co-workers and strangers with whom you already have a nodding acquaintance.

• When you use drive-up windows that have those pneumatic tubes, put a pack of sugarless gum into the tube before you send it in.

• Write "thank you" notes for everything under the sun. Make a commitment to express your gratitude when...
   * you've been entertained at another's home,
   * you've received a gift of any size,
   * you've been comforted through a rough time,
   * someone has done you a favor,
   * businesses have served you well,
   * you've shared a fun experience with another person,
   * you've received good advice,
   * those you love have been helped by someone else,
   * and when you are reminded of just how important someone is to you. For example, think about people from your past who taught you important lessons about yourself, about life, or about some other important issue.
   Always keep plenty of notes and stamps handy, and write the note immediately. Don't wait for poetic inspiration. Just say "Thanks so much for...." And as soon as you seal the envelope, get the note off your desk and into your mailbox for the next mail delivery/pick-up.

• Looking for a good excuse to be playful and kind? Here are some national holidays that are especially noteworthy for Kindness Guerrillas... and anyone else who likes to play:

* Fourth Tuesday in January: Clash Day (wear mismatched clothes)
* February 14th: Valentine's Day
* March 22nd: National Goof-Off Day
* April 1st: April Fool's Day
* April 28th: Kiss-Your-Mate Day
* Second Sunday in May: Mother's Day
* Third Sunday in June: Father's Day
* July 11th: Cheer-Up-The-Lonely Day
* First Sunday in August: Friendship Day
* September 15th: Respect For The Aged Day
* First Sunday in October: Grandparents' Day
* October 19th: Sweetest Day (give sweet treats)
* November 11th: Remembrance Day.

Some people make their own holidays, their own excuses to be playful. I have different friends who celebrate the Ides of March, summer and winter solstice, spring equinox, Millard Fillmore's birthday, Robert E. Lee's birthday, the Persieds meteor shower, Shrove Tuesday (Mardi gras), and May Day.

• Dave opened my eyes. A paraplegic, Dave complains that most people with obvious disabilities are treated as though they're invisible. People don't want to stare and end up overcompensating. "Tell people," Dave urges me, "not to be afraid to ask, 'Why are you in that chair?' or 'How long have you have those braces?' Don't overdo the sympathy. Lead the conversation away from the handicap to the other day-to-day issues other folks talk about."

Thanks, Dave.

• Hide loving notes in your kids' books, binders, and lunch pails for them to find at school.

In an informal survey of my students each semester, I've asked "What are some of the most loving things your parents did for you?" Almost every semester there has been one student who has mentioned this specific kindness. And everyone else has said "Neat. I wish my parents had done that for me."

• Do you remember how relieved you felt when you discovered that an article you misplaced had been turned in to the Lost & Found? Make the effort to locate the Lost & Found when you come across things others have lost. If the object has a name on it, call the person to tell her where she can find the missing whatever.

GUERRILLA TIP

Imagine.

It's amazing how much you can discover about others if you put on your detective cap, fire up your imagination, and place yourself in others' shoes. You'll find you can almost always come up with practical answers to the question, "What can I do or say right now that would make that person happy?" It may be a smile... a kind word... holding a door open... making a call... or dropping a simple note in the mail. But the key is imagining — making guesses as to what others may be thinking or feeling — and then imagining how you can tailor your words or deeds to please them.

> *If you want to enlarge that mystic organ whence flows true human kindness, you must cultivate your imagination. You must learn to put yourself in another's place, think his thoughts.*
>
> — Frank Gelett Burgess

• Keep a box of LifeSavers — each roll tied with a brightly colored bow — around the house. They're handy for spur-of-the-moment "thank you's" for the various service people who come by your home: the meter reader, the Mail Carrier, the trash collectors, the UPS driver, people selling things or collecting for non-profit groups, the police patrol, the paper delivery person. I also keep LifeSavers in my briefcase, my fanny pack, and my car. That way I'm prepared to surprise and thank people wherever I go.

• The end of a fun vacation is depressing, isn't it? When neighbors are due to return from vacation, put a festive "Welcome Home" note on their door. If you're home when they return, order a large pizza to be delivered to your home then take it over for them; they will be tired and will probably appreciate not having to prepare a meal.

• The most likeable person I know is David, a former student. He is so... how to say it... he PRESUMES THE BEST! When we're throwing Frisbees in the park, for example, he always looks around to see if there are others who might want to be included. Then, he doesn't ask them. He throws them the Frisbee.

GUERRILLA TIP

Start early in the day.

In the first part of this century, early Kindness Guerrilla David Dunn wrote a charming book called *Try Giving Yourself Away*. In his book, Dunn tells about how he discovered the value of starting the day off with a kind word or deed. When you perform a kind act early in the day, you have the entire day to enjoy the after-glow. And when still glowing, Dunn notes, you're more likely to notice other opportunities to do small kindnesses.

Warmly greeting your family at breakfast is a good way to start the day. You may also decide to greet the first stranger you pass with a smile and a cheerful "Good Morning." Be unusually courteous in rush-hour traffic. Or, notice and compliment the first friends or co-workers you see on what they're wearing.

• Those huge mega-hardware stores that carry lumber and other building supplies are fertile ground for Kindness Guerrillas. Do a 360-degree sweep of the parking lot with your eyes, and you'll sometimes see someone struggling to load or unload a car. Check out the lot at the grocery and other stores, too. Every now and then you'll find that you can assist others in loading their purchases into their cars. Keep a special eye out for the elderly, people with small children, and the handicapped.

• Promote the kindness revolution in your corner of the world with this small act of generous nonsense: before leaving a coffee shop, secretly pay for someone else's coffee. They'll be delighted and mystified all day.

• Groups frighten some people. They find it impossible to chime into discussions in even casual gatherings. Many such people, however, will talk if explicitly invited to join in. Keep an eye out for quiet members in your group; when there's a lull, ask them general questions about their thoughts or feelings regarding the topic. Just "What do you think about the issue, Paul?" is often enough of an invitation.

• Ever feel smothered? Each of us needs to receive and give space. All of us need solitude to recharge our batteries. Sometimes others are able to be aware of and communicate their needs. Sometimes not. Be sensitive to when friends or family may be feeling crowded and tactfully arrange to give them some time alone.

• I recognized him. Stooped shoulders, wearing a wool hat, carrying his ubiquitous shopping bag, and shuffling along a busy road — he was a neighborhood character. I had the impulse to stop and offer him a ride home, and he accepted.

Mr. Leznikowski, it turned out, had been a jeweler and gem cutter and had once lived in our house. When arthritis forced him to give up his trade, he moved to a small apartment in the neighborhood. The ride was short, but we sat in the car in front of his home and talked. He told me about his memories of living where we live, his homeland (Poland), and his many years as a jeweler. I could tell he was delighted to describe the time he was called on to cut a four carat diamond!

If you see someone walking down the sidewalk with an armload of grocery bags, stop and offer a ride home.

- A guerrilla classic: pay the toll of the car behind you at toll booths. This act of random kindness is sure to put a smile on your face. It's fun to imagine what the receivers of your gift made of this peculiar good fortune.

- When you come across an obstacle lying in the street, stop and move it out of the roadway. Someone has to do it, and you may be the only Kindness Guerrilla on that stretch of road.

- My mom let me know I was treasured. Whenever we were reading, watching TV, or engaged in some other passive activity, she would touch me: hold my hands, let me put my head in her lap, or just sit shoulder to shoulder. Her touch always made me feel safe, secure, and loved.

- "Live simply so others may simply live." That motto fits my friend Kyle. So does the button he sometimes wears: "LOVE PEOPLE. USE THINGS." Kyle earns a handsome salary as a chemical engineer, but his lifestyle is modest. Instead of a classy home, flashy car, and expensive toys, Kyle uses his resources to help sponsor organizations that assist people in need: a free medical clinic, a food pantry, a shelter for the homeless, and an after-school program for kids from the inner city.

GUERRILLA TIP

Act when feeling down.

Almost all of us have discovered that helping can be a powerful anti-depressant. And there's plenty of scientific support for the curative power of doing good.

Put Dr. Karl Menninger's formula on your icebox for the next time you're feeling down. Include the formula in your note to a friend who is feeling blue. MENNINGER'S 10 RULES TO CURE THE BLUES: "Do something for someone else. Repeat 9X."

If you want others to be happy, practice compassion. If you want to be happy, practice compassion.
— the Dalai Lama

• Peter has blocked out 20 minutes a day to respond to messages. No mail or phone messages lie on his desk more than 24 hours. Peter believes it's an important courtesy to promptly answer letters and return calls.

• Learn CPR and the Heimlich Maneuver.

• Think of animals as fellow travelers in our earth journey, and treat them with kindness. Wild birds need water in the summer, and food for the winter and spring. Our dogs and cats need affectionate attention from us: quality time when they're stroked and played with. Never purposely injure an animal.

• Mason found a dollar bill in the bible placed in his motel room. Clipped to the bill was a note directing him to the mystery giver's favorite verse. "I hope it will help you too," the note concluded. Mason told me he hadn't realized how depressed he was until he read the verse. He cried. And the verse did help him.
Leave a dollar and a note in a motel bible, and leave the rest to God.

18,000 WAYS TO BE KIND

I hope the ideas you're reading about in *Guerrilla Kindness* have started you thinking creatively about other options. Creativity is the key. Most of the opportunities for kindness that develop before our eyes require us to notice them, improvise a way to respond, and act — all on our own, on the spot, and without hesitation.

The chart on the following pages should challenge your imagination. Pick items from each list, put them together, and see if you can discover new kindnesses to try. For example, pick "public space/transportation terminal" from *Place*, "physical help" and "information" from *Gift*, and "elderly" from *Recipient*. What possible kindnesses come to mind? Lifting an elderly person's heavy bag from the conveyor belt at the airport and pointing out a porter to haul it to the taxi stand; that's one possibility. Or helping an elderly person up the stairs onto a bus and, after finding his or her destination, advising about the right stop to get off the bus.

Over 9,000 combinations of Place, Gift, and Recipient are possible, each with many variations. Assuming just two variations for each combination, we have 18,000 occasions to act kindly.

PLACE Pick One	GIFT Pick One Or More	RECIPIENT Pick One
1. home	1. courtesy	1. family
2. other's home	2. a favor	2. neighbor
3. neighborhood	3. skill/ability	3. friend
4. recreation location	4. information	4. motorist
5. health facility	5. companionship	5. traveler
6. shop/mall	6. a material gift	6. elderly
7. repair center	7. physical help	7. kids
8. workplace	8. a compliment	8. handicapped or infirmed
9. church	9. appreciation	9. non-profit agency
10. service agency	10. beauty	10. bosses/managers

PLACE	GIFT	RECIPIENT
11. business location	11. respect	11. professionals
12. lodging	12. time	12. stranger/others
13. restaurant	13. energy	13. co-workers
14. car	14. interest and attention	14. those confined
15. public space	15. understanding	15. service personnel
parks	16. encouragement	receptionists
roadways	17. tolerance	trades workers
sidewalks	18. kindness	people who wait
buildings	19. entertainment	on you
on water	20. warmth/affection	federal, state
parking lots	21. money	or local
public facilities		government
public transportation		employees
travel terminals		

GUERRILLA WORKS

- I never would have thought of it, but Leela showed me how you can put money into others' pockets without taking a cent from your own. Clip all coupons for the grocery you use. For those items you don't want, place the coupons on the shelves in front of the products for which the coupon is good.

- I don't hesitate to say, "Can I help you find what you're looking for." Even if I'm as lost as the other person seems to be. I know that it's a comfort not to be lost by yourself. If you see someone at a grocery, shopping center, or office building who seems to be lost, ask if you can help whether or not you're familiar with the place.

- Produce a "radio show" for a friend who has moved away and may be homesick. When Lorraine moved, her friends got together, gathered music they knew she liked, and recorded a 90-minute cassette. Their radio show featured music and a different person talking between each song. They called their program "This Is Dedicated To The One We Love."

• Teach youngsters to become more aware of Mother Earth. Invite them to care for life. Just before May Day send packs of flower seeds to each of your favorite young friends. Marigolds and pincushion flowers are great choices. They're simple to grow, bloom all the way to Fall, and love to be cut for bouquets.

• I've made lots of mistakes. My friend Ed, however, continues to respect the choices I make. He doesn't say, "Oh Gavin, I wouldn't do that. Remember what happened the last time you...." Ed respects my right to make and learn from my mistakes.

Psychologist Keith Davis has studied the characteristics of friendship and found that good friends demonstrate their mutual respect when each assumes the other will exercise good judgement in making choices. When I read Davis's article in *Psychology Today*, I immediately thought of my friend Ed.

Find something positive and enthusiastic to say about the things others are planning to do. Be among those rare, kind friends who *respect others' rights to make their own decisions* even if they believe those decisions are foolish, uninformed, or mistaken.

GUERRILLA TIP

Be kind to the guerrilla.

What makes a kind person? It's a fact: people who have a positive view of themselves are more likely to view others positively. Kindness begins with yourself.

The problem is that most of us have an unfairly negative self-concept. And we maintain that negative view by discounting the good things we do and exaggerating the bad. To be a Kindness Guerrilla you need to work daily to raise your self-esteem.

Make a note of the caring things you do. Be aware of each kind deed and kind word, and remember them. Tell others about them. Keep a journal. There's even proof of your good intentions in your hands right now: you're reading a book about how to become a kinder person!

It's reasonable and right for you to be gentle with yourself. Acknowledge your deep-down goodness. Start right now.

• It's the best answer I received to question #1 on my informal survey of secondary school teachers. The question: "How do you manage to keep your patience?" The answer: "I keep my sense of humor in trying situations by telling myself, 'This is actually all being taped by Candid Camera,' and then I behave like I would like to see myself behaving if I were on national TV."

• Carry pre-stamped, pre-addressed stationery with you. In stray moments — sitting in waiting rooms, after a meal at a restaurant, or when traveling — jot a few lines to someone you've been meaning to write. The letter written on the run! You won't have as many wasted minutes in your life... and your friends will enjoy hearing from you more often.

• Friends who live in the country ask us to give them our bagged leaves and grass. They use the huge mound of material they receive to build a compost pile. Tom and Jessie water and turn the compost pile every few weeks.
In the spring, they use the same bags in which they received the raw materials to deliver a great soil conditioner to all of us city folks who have gardens.

• In a crowded airport, train or bus station, or waiting room, volunteer to change seats so that a family can sit together.

GUERRILLA TIP

Do it three times.

When experimenting with a new kindness, do it three times. The first time to get past most of the discomfort; the second to learn how to do it; and the third to decide if you like it.

A campaign of Guerrilla Kindness is easy to sustain once you've gotten over the awkwardness that all of us feel when experimenting. Saying a kind word to a stranger, for example, is scary at first. But when you see — AND YOU WILL SEE — the almost magical power you have to instantly brighten others' faces, you'll be encouraged to continue. The power of Guerrilla Kindness is truly awesome!

> *Kind words are the music of the world. They have a power which seems to be beyond natural causes, as though they were some angel's song which had lost its way and come down to earth.*
>
> — Frederick W. Faber

- Do you sometimes run out of ideas to keep kids busy on long rides in the car? Next trip, tell the kids you'll give them a nickel for every other traveler they can get to wave back to them.

- If you're in good health, stand up when being introduced and, even, when meeting a friend. The pleasure of seeing another person stand up just for us is practically universal, and it's an easy way to make others feel more important.

- Practice acts of senseless beauty. Throw rainbows over your ceiling and walls by putting a reflector in a sunny window. Learn to play the recorder. Hang a windsock or windchimes from your porch. Take a class in calligraphy. Perfume a home or office with a bouquet of gardenias.

- One present that's always well received is a gift certificate from your friend's favorite store. Besides the joy of the gift itself, your friend has the pleasure of browsing in a place that's special to him or her.

- Find something you like or respect in others and let them know.

This simple Guerrilla Work is more difficult than it seems at first. Almost everyone agrees the world would be a much warmer place if we all did it, but... HOW DO YOU DO IT?

In the 1936 classic, *How To Win Friends And Influence People,* Dale Carnegie tells about the time he was stuck in a long line at the post office. As the postal clerk was handling each customer's business — weighing envelopes, counting out stamps, making change — Carnegie was struck with how monumentally bored the man must be. Carnegie decided he wanted to brighten the clerk's day so he asked himself the question, "What is there about him that I can honestly admire?" By the time his turn had come, Dale Carnegie had a compliment that left the clerk radiating with pleasure.

I've used that question for years and never failed to come up with an answer. Ask yourself, "What is there about that person I can genuinely admire?" and you'll always have an honest, kind word for those who look like they need a touch of Guerrilla Kindness.

(The 1988 revision of *How To Win Friends And Influence People* is available from Simon and Schuster, $5.99)

- The instant you feel yourself becoming defensive, agree with the person who is criticizing you.

This revolutionary response is easier than it seems. You'll find that you can always agree in one of two ways with a critic. First, agree with only that portion of the complaint that's true. Most of the time there is some truth to what others say about us. "You're right. I may sometimes do that."

If nothing's true, exercise option two: agree with their right to their opinion. "If I saw things the way you do, I think I would probably feel exactly the same way." Which, if you think about it, is true.

In either case, your unexpected response will both disarm your critic and reduce your own defensiveness.

- If friends are flying out of town, volunteer to drive them and pick them up at the airport so they don't have to pay a taxi or for parking. Plus, it's nice to have someone meet us when we come home.

- Get neighbors together for an alley clean-up. Your city's Board of Public Works may send a truck to haul off the trash you pick-up. Afterwards, enjoy a neighborhood cookout and get to know your neighbors better.

GUERRILLA TIP

Form a Guerrilla Group.

Friends may enjoy getting together regularly to hear others' ideas and stories of specific kindnesses each has done since the last get-together.

And you'll find that it's easier to stay enthusiastic and imaginative when you have a support group. Guerrilla Groups are great for brainstorming — "whacking each other on the side of the head" (as Roger von Oech says in his book on creativity, *A Whack On The Side Of The Head*) — and coming up with novel Guerrilla Works to surprise and delight others.

My Guerrilla Group is Patchwork: the community of friends with whom I worship. Our group brainstormed for acts of Guerrilla Kindness to help me prepare this book. And still, almost every Sunday, someone will come to me with a new kindness dreamt up during the past week.

- Talk to someone whose opinion on some matter is different from yours. Ask her to explain why she thinks as she does. Suspend your judgment, and really try to understand. See if you can paraphrase — to her satisfaction — what you think her view is. You may be surprised to discover more common ground than you had anticipated.

- Repeat your congratulations. Complimenting someone right after a good job is just paying dues, doing the expected. But waiting a few days or weeks — when others will expect you to have forgotten the accomplishment — and praising them again... will *turn a mere courtesy into a lasting feeling of warmth and pride.*

- Teach a child to feel at home under the stars.

Every summer Niles and Suzanne take a group of Scouts out into the country to learn the night sky. They marvel at the Milky Way, watch how the Scorpion chases the Hunter, and, by the end of the evening, each youngster knows how to find the North Star using the Big Dipper and Cassiopeia.

On August 12th, take a group out to the country to watch the summer's most spectacular stellar event, the Perseids Meteor Shower. On December 13th, the Geminids Meteor Shower matches the Perseids display with 50 shooting stars every hour!

GUERRILLA TIP

Touch the lives of 20,454 people.

If, at age 21, you start smiling, saying "Hi," and complimenting a different person each day, you will have made 20,454 lives breath a bit easier by the time you are 75 — the average American life span. If you begin at 30, you can put smiles on 17,021 faces. And even if you wait til 40, you can brighten a day for 13,253 people.

> *In a thousand ways life gains sweetness through the consciousness of the ability to do small kindnesses, to render minor services, to exercise a little thoughtfulness and courtesy.*
>
> — Hamilton Wright Mabie

- Organize some event — a celebration, songfest, work project, or worship service — between your church and another church of a different denomination.

- Eleanor calls the people who listen to complaints all day. She calls corporations, government agencies, schools, and, of course, the newspapers: "May I speak with the person who handles complaints?" she asks. She knows how she wants to start her conversations — thanking the patience people for their service — but she doesn't plan anything beyond that. "I want to listen. That's all. And once they know I'm on their side, my new friends pour out their hearts." Her conversations almost always last for at least 20 minutes and range from philosophy and religion and politics to personal stories about family and friends. "People ask me to call them back. And I do. How could I not? We have such wonderful talks."

- Can small change make a big difference? Take a chance and press a gift into every needy hand outstretched to you. You never know what hope your gifts may restore.

- The first and last word in kindness is the Golden Rule.

CONCLUSION

*Life is short and we have not too much time for gladdening
the hearts of those who are traveling the dark way with us.
Oh, be swift to love! Make haste to be kind.*

— Henri Amiel

This is not an ending. Today is the first day of the rest of our lives (as the saying goes). Today we can launch a lifetime commitment to act on the kind and generous impulses we each have. We join the expanding guerrilla force dedicated to overcoming the domination of the profit motive with lives motivated instead by kindheartedness. We begin our celebration of the new millennium early by stepping out and acting as if the global village already is what we hope it will become: a family whose first order of concern is for each other's welfare.

Reading *Guerrilla Kindness* and looking for opportunities to be kind has sparked your imagination, I hope, and you have discovered many more ways to show kindness than are suggested here. Please write me, tell me the kindnesses you've discovered, and help make the next edition of this book twice as large as this one. Write me in care of Impact Publishers, Post Office Box 1094, San Luis Obispo, California 93406-1094.

Have you had a kindness shown?
Pass it on;
'Twas not given for thee alone,
Pass it on;
Let it travel down the years,
Let it wipe another's tears,
'Till in Heaven the deed appears —
Pass it on.

— Henry Burton

APPENDIX

"Patchwork Central"

*Seek the welfare of any city to which I have carried you off,
and pray to God for it; for in its welfare you will find your
welfare.*

— Jeremiah 29:7

Patchwork is an intentional community of men and women of many ages, races, faiths, and political views. Although we maintain a variety of separate professional careers, we worship and play together. And all of us devote important parts of our lives to minister to the inner-city residents of Evansville, Indiana. It is our intention to respond to the needs of this place as best we can out of the gifts, resources, and training with which we have been blessed.

Our active ministries have changed a lot since 1977 when we made our first convenant to serve our neighbors. In the years since, we've helped provide jobs, food, clothing, housing, dental and medical care, financial assistance to small businesses, after-school children's programs, meeting and office space, art, adult education, entertainment, fellowship, and welcome.

Patchwork Central is supported by volunteers and financial contributions from friends all over the country. Your purchase of *Guerrilla Kindness* will help sustain our work.

For more information, write us at:

Patchwork Central
100 Washington Avenue
Evansville, Indiana 47713